TWO VOYAGERS
AT THE COURT OF KING ALFRED

The ventures of OHTHERE and WULFSTAN
together with the
Description of Northern Europe
from the
OLD ENGLISH OROSIUS

edited by
Niels Lund

translated by
Christine E. Fell

with contributory essays by
Ole Crumlin-Pedersen
P. H. Sawyer
Christine E. Fell

William Sessions Limited
YORK, ENGLAND

First published in 1984

ISBN 0 900657 86 3

An English-language companion volume
to the Danish *Ottar og Wulfstan*
(published at Roskilde in 1983).

*The printing of this edition of the voyages of
Ohthere and Wulfstan has been financed by the
Sessions Book Trust and has also been made
possible by a gift to the University of Cambridge
in memory of Dorothea Coke, Skjæret, 1951.*

The Authors

Dr Niels Lund is a Senior Lecturer in Medieval History at the University of Copenhagen.
Ole Crumlin-Pedersen is head of the Institute of Maritime Archaeology in Roskilde.
Christine Fell is Professor of Early English Studies at the University of Nottingham.
Peter Sawyer, formerly Professor of Medieval History, is now Senior Fellow at the University of Leeds.

*The cover picture shows Odin's Raven, the famous replica of a Viking longship which Robin Bigland commissioned in 1979
to celebrate the Manx millennium. Robin's crew navigated Odin's Raven across the North Sea from Norway to Britain, just
as the Norwegian sailor Ohthere set out for the court of King Alfred with his cargo of walrus ivory a thousand years ago. We
are deeply grateful to Robin Bigland for his permission to use this photograph.*

Contents

Principal Illustrations

Foreword

By Sir David Wilson, Director of The British Museum

The record of voyages made by two merchant venturers Ohthere and Wulfstan in the time of King Alfred is one of our most exciting and important primary sources for this period, not only for Anglo-Saxon England but also for Scandinavia and the Baltic in the Viking Age. It is a text so packed with information that it has needed a team of four scholars to produce this edition and commentary, drawing on all the discoveries of recent scholarship. Niels Lund, a distinguished Danish historian, has provided the edition and his compatriot Ole Crumlin-Pedersen has drawn on his detailed knowledge of ships and navigation for his contributory essay. The English scholars in the team, Peter Sawyer and Christine Fell, have added essays on the trading background and the language problems. It is a work that has long needed doing.

David M. Wilson

Introduction

Ohthere's accounts of his voyages from northern Norway are some of the most frequently cited texts from the Viking Age. He lived somewhere near Tromsø, and travelled from there both northwards round North Cape into the White Sea, and southwards to the market-place *Sciringesheal*, later known as Kaupang, in the Oslo-fjord, and further on to Hedeby near Schleswig. His accounts together with one by another merchant called Wulfstan, of a journey from Hedeby to Truso in present day Poland, have survived in a surprising context, namely in a translation into Old English of the *Seven Books of History against the Pagans, Historiarum adversum Paganos Libri Septem*, by the Spanish churchman Paulus Orosius.

Orosius' work is a history of the world from the Creation until AD 417 and the peculiar title is explained by the political situation that gave Orosius cause to write it. About AD 400 Rome's greatness had long since faded, many provinces had been abandoned, as Britain was soon to be, to the barbarians who in the Migration period were flooding Europe and settling in many places. The Empire had been split in two in AD 395 and not even the Italian peninsula could be defended against them anymore. In AD 410 the unimaginable disaster took place: on the 24th of August Rome itself was captured by the Visigoths under Alaric and pillaged for three days. The inconceivable had occurred and this inevitably invited profound reflection.

It was a widely held opinion that this disaster and many others were the revenge of the ancient gods for the apostasy. A hundred years earlier in AD 313 Constantine the Great had granted freedom of worship in the Western Empire so that Christians would no longer suffer martyrdom for sticking to their faith, and in AD 380 Christianity had been made the State religion and Jove with all the other ancient gods had been sent packing. But this was only thirty years before Rome fell and the old gods were still remembered by many people who now interpreted these disasters as divine revenge for desertion and advocated their restoration to avert further disaster.

The Christians, of course, were bound to refute these arguments and many theologians took up the pen to contribute to the discussion. Orosius was to contribute a short, concise history of the world listing all those disasters, wars, natural catastrophes, etc. which the ancient gods had not averted in those centuries when they were in unrivalled power. Orosius was encouraged to write this work by his mentor, Bishop Augustine of Hippo, whose own contribution eventually became one of the most influential and important books of the Middle Ages: *De Civitate Dei, The City of God*.

The *Seven Books* of Orosius is no great achievement. From the point of view of his own time as well as from that of posterity it is a mediocre one. He availed himself of a rather limited selection of sources, and most of these are known to us. One observation made by Orosius, however, had great importance for medieval political thinking: that of the four empires succeeding each other from east to west, the fourth of which, the Roman Empire, was to be the last and to stand until the coming of Antichrist.

By the ninth century Orosius' world history had become a classic and it was none other than King Alfred the Great who caused it to be translated into Old English. It has been believed until recently that William of Malmesbury was right in ascribing the translation to the king himself but scholars have now cast doubt on this theory. Alfred had become king of Wessex in 871, the only Anglo-Saxon kingdom not conquered by the Vikings. His rule began with a long succession of battles against this enemy and he did well enough to be able to buy peace from them before winter. Seven years later Wessex very nearly succumbed to the Vikings; many of the leading men submitted to them and paid homage to their leaders while Alfred himself was roaming about the woods and moors with a small following of faithful men. In the end, however, Alfred came out of the woods with sufficient strength to beat the enemies and their leader Guthrum accepted baptism together with thirty leading men of the army, Alfred standing sponsor.

Map of England in the time of King Alfred.
In Anglo-Saxon times England did not form one kingdom; it was divided up into a varying number of small kingdoms trying to achieve supremacy over each other. In the beginning of the ninth century there were four kingdoms: Wessex, Mercia, East Anglia and Northumbria but by the end of it Northumbria, East Anglia and the eastern part of Mercia had fallen to the Vikings who established kingdoms in East Anglia and York while Mercia was split up into a number of earldoms with centres like the Five Boroughs; Lincoln, Stamford, Leicester, Nottingham and Derby. Wessex successfully resisted the Viking onslaught and was able to retain its independence and to establish some form of overlordship over English Mercia, whose ealdorman was King Alfred's son-in-law. In 886 a treaty was concluded between King Alfred and the Danish King Guthrum of East Anglia which among other things drew up the boundary between the two kingdoms: 'First as to the boundaries between us: up the Thames, and up the Lea, and along the Lea to its source, then in a straight line to Bedford, and then up the Ouse to Watling Street'. Watling Street, the present A5, formed the boundary between the Danelaw and the rest of England.

Having achieved this, Alfred devoted all his resources to the regeneration of his country and to the fortification of it against future attacks. He is venerated as the founder of the Royal Navy, he reformed civil and military organisation and he created a system of boroughs serving as strongholds for the local population. His efforts proved very successful. When a new Viking army attacked in 892 they had a much more difficult time than previously.

Alfred sought the model for many of his reforms across the Channel in Frankia and from here too came the inspiration for his cultural activity. In addition to the reforms already mentioned, Alfred attached great importance to a cultural restoration of his country and he patterned his work on nothing less than the Carolingian Renaissance, that extensive study of classical authors which Charlemagne initiated at his court in Aix-la-Chapelle and for which he gathered around him a number of scholars, such as Alcuin, who came from York.

Providing translations was an important part of Alfred's cultural effort, since the knowledge of Latin was restricted to narrowly limited circles of the population: but while Charlemagne encouraged his scholars to work on classical literature, Alfred chose theological works, the Fathers of the Church and others. He translated, possibly with the help of others, Gregory the Great's *Cura Pastoralis*, a manual for bishops on how to discharge their office well, St Augustine's *Soliloquia*, and Boethius's *De Consolatione Philosophiæ*.

At the same time vernacular surveys appear both of English history and of world history. For a history of England, Bede's *Ecclesiastical History of the English People* was the obvious choice; this goes as far as 731 and to supplement it the *Anglo-Saxon Chronicle* was compiled. For a world history Orosius' *Seven Books against the Pagans*, which had in the meantime become a standard work, was an equally obvious choice.

Orosius' history begins with a geographical survey of the world, that is as much of it as he knew, but in the English version this was extended to include a description of areas not dealt with by Orosius, namely Europe north of the Alps. The description of Northern Europe translated here is therefore an original piece of work from the late ninth century, not a translation of Orosius.

If the description is original, what sources were used? Does it provide primary information or did the author draw from sources also available today? In the latter case we would have a chance to check him and to assess his reliability.

We can gain some impression of his working method and his reading, through an analysis of his translation of Orosius' text. This proves to be very free. He tacitly corrects, supplements and explains freely, and we can trace the sources on which he drew for these purposes. The translator reveals himself as a very learned man with a profound knowledge of classical literature as well as of the literature after Orosius. This knowledge and learning must be expected to influence his treatment of northern Europe and much of the information given here is in fact traceable to Pliny, possibly through the widely read *Etymologies* written before AD 636 by Isidore of Seville. We are not justified in assuming, therefore, that the information supplied in this part of the work was contemporary or was still correct when it was compiled in the last decade of the ninth century. The mention of such phenomena as the Riphæan Mountains and Land of the Women clearly depends on literary tradition, and the reference to the Dacians, who were Goths, similarly depends on obsolete book-learning.

It has been suggested that the list of the many tribes in central and eastern Europe, some of whom were very small, was based on a map of the world. This, however, would presuppose access to a much more detailed map than is known to have existed in the early Middle Ages. Contemporary maps of the world were limited to much broader outlines, and ideas of what the world was like were very imprecise.

Not all the information, however, could come from classical authors; the Slav expansion took place in the Dark Ages and was not completed until about AD 600, and the information about the location of their numerous tribes is therefore likely to have been fairly recent if not contemporary. The likely sources were people who had travelled among them or perhaps the Franks, for the Slavs, the Sorbs, the Siusli, etc., were their neighbours and Charlemagne had established the *limes sorabicus* against them. They are frequently mentioned in the East Frankish annals. It should not be forgotten that, in spite of the Viking activity and other perils, lively mercantile and cultural contacts were maintained on the continent as well as with England. Much travel took place, surprisingly much. Many descriptions of Viking activity create the impression that for two centuries the Vikings laid claim to virtually all the attention of western Europe but if the accounts of the Vikings are read in their context, and thus seen in their proper perspective, it becomes clear that the Franks and often even the English were preoccupied by more important problems. It is also clear that many journeys were made across Europe despite the Vikings. *The Anglo-Saxon Chronicle* records that in 889 there was no expedition to Rome, only carriers were sent with letters. It may be inferred that in normal years there was an expedition to Rome. Alfred, indeed, had visited Rome as a child and his father Æthelwulf, King of Wessex, spent a full year there in 855-856, and on his way home gained a daughter of the Frankish King Charles the Bald as his queen. That *Chronicle* was compiled at the same time and in the same circles as the Orosius-translation and it incorporates much accurate information about contemporary Frankia.

It was possible, then, for the learned entourage of King Alfred to acquire information about conditions and events on the continent from travellers as well as from other sources. The accounts of the journeys of Ohthere and Wulfstan

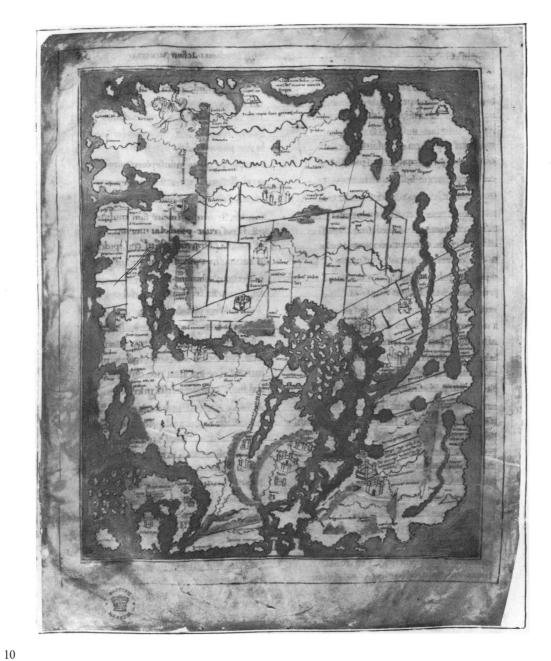

10

that follow the description of northern Europe are examples of the use of information provided by travellers. The reason their information has not been integrated into the description is probably that it was so special that it could not be compared or combined with information from other sources.

It should be remembered, though, that even if these accounts appear to be the words of Ohthere and Wulfstan themselves – and are often used as though they were – they have in fact been taken down and adapted by others. We may imagine that when Ohthere arrived in Wessex, a rich chieftain from an exotic part of the world, he was invited to the court and that he contributed to the entertainment on more than one occasion for those present, who included the scholars King Alfred had gathered around him. The information supplied about Ohthere's wealth probably shows us in a glimpse how the conversation developed. Ohthere told his audience that he was among the chief men in his country and immediately they wanted to know how many cows, sheep and pigs he owned and how much land he ploughed; this was the measure of wealth among them. And since by that standard his wealth was far from impressive they required him to explain what his wealth consisted of.

One of the scholars present may have taken notes of Ohthere's account intending to utilize it in his introduction to Orosius, and he may afterwards have spoken to Ohthere alone to make sure he had got all these strange things right, for there were undoubtedly some language difficulties to overcome. He later adapted it to suit his own readership, and the inveterate teacher shines through when he associates the unknown with something familiar. Thus it was hardly Ohthere himself who, when mentioning Jutland and *Sillende*, informed his hosts that 'the Angles lived in these districts before they came to this land'. This is the comment of an English author for the benefit of an English audience already familiar with Bede's *History*. The information about the lands on Ohthere's starboard when sailing south along the Norwegian coast is probably of the same character. Neither Ireland, the Orkneys, the Hebrides nor Britain could be seen from Ohthere's ship but mentioning them helps an Englishman's understanding of the text.

It has been suggested, however, that what is indicated is the sequence of the points of departure of the sea-routes to Ireland, the Orkneys, etc. If this is the correct interpretation it might strengthen the argument for reading Iceland instead of Ireland. This emendation has been suggested and if the text is read with a modern map in mind there seems to be a good case for it. However, neither Ohthere nor the English author of this account had such a map so that their world looked entirely different from ours. They imagined the continent to be an island surrounded by an ocean in which there were also some islands, – like Britain and, in the far north, Thule – but of the location of these islands in relation to the continent they had only the vaguest of ideas. One should also remember that when Ohthere visited Wessex, Iceland was very recently discovered and might never have been heard of in southwest England.

Another reason for emending Ireland to Iceland has been found in the 'erroneous' location of Ireland north of Britain. It is questionable, however, how erroneous this location is. On a modern map, of course, Ireland is to the west of Britain but leaving this out of account and taking our point of departure in Wessex it seems perfectly reasonable to consider Ireland a locality to the north, the journey there is largely northbound, and according to older maps Ireland seems to have been looked upon as an island one step further out in the ocean than Britain, *i.e.* further to the north.

This problem leads into the discussion about the points of the compass in the Old English Orosius. Some scholars have maintained that the north of that time deviated by up to 60° clockwise from our north, and that therefore no emendation is required. This would place Ireland more to the north of Britain and it would render more acceptable many indications of direction on the continent, including the odd location of south Danes and north Danes in relation to each other. A very lengthy discussion has been conducted on this subject but conclusive arguments in favour of such deviation have not been produced. In most cases a simpler explanation is available.

Ohthere's account shows more traces of the vague cosmological ideas of that day. The English interviewer was clearly very interested in solving a problem that interested him but which Ohthere, unaware of the classical world picture, could hardly ever have considered. The English scholar was very anxious to find out whether Ohthere had been travelling along the utmost edge of the continent or whether there was land even further north than he had been. It is therefore important for him, when Ohthere changes direction, to establish whether the land is turning or the sea is penetrating the land. On the face of it one would consider this a meaningless question but if the land is turning Ohthere is at the edge of the world, if the sea is penetrating the land he is merely entering another sea like the Mediterranean or the Baltic.

In the text Alfred is styled Ohthere's lord, his *hlaford*. What kind of relationship in fact existed between the two is somewhat enigmatic. We do not know how long Ohthere spent at the king's court. Rasmus Rask, who edited the text with a Danish translation in 1815, construed him as an exile who had been driven away from Norway by Harald Fairhair but the whole context seems to suggest that he could hardly have spent more than one or two summer months in Wessex. There is no indication that he had lost his wealth at home nor that he did not intend to return to sell his 600 unsold reindeer. Ohthere therefore seems unlikely to have entered the service of King Alfred or to have become his retainer in the normal sense of the word. A *hlaford* was the lord of his men in the sense that they owed him allegiance and service, in return he owed them protection, *mund*, and sometimes stipend and keep. The key to their relationship perhaps lies in the concept of *mund*. Any Englishman visiting the court of Alfred would have a lord and thus a protector who could help protect his rights if he became involved in a dispute. In the towns, guilds offered equivalent protection but people travelling abroad had no protection and technically speaking they were 'outlaws'. Their sole protector was the king who was, by virtue of his office, protector of strangers, and from that point of view he might be considered lord of strangers and foreigners. Therefore foreigners were required to pay dues to the king; Ohthere, as we are told, gave the king some precious walrus ivory. If Ohthere was in fact a guest at court and not just another merchant visiting the country it may have seemed natural to style Alfred as his lord.

The text of the Old English Orosius has been handed down to us in two manuscripts, one of which is contemporary. This is the *Tollemache Orosius* (MS BL Additional 47967) which was probably written in Winchester by a scribe who also worked on the Parker manuscript of the *Anglo-Saxon Chronicle* between 892 and 924. This manuscript is complete except for folios 9-16 and those unfortunately contained most of Ohthere and the whole of Wulfstan. This lacuna was filled in the seventeenth century from an eleventh-century manuscript, MS BL Cotton Tiberius B i. These manuscripts are very close to each other, differences between them being insignificant and the lacuna in the *Tollemache Orosius* is therefore no catastrophe for the transmission of the text. Both manuscripts are now in the British Library and a facsimile has been published of the older of them. The first modern edition was published by D. Barrington in 1773, and the most recent modern edition is that of Janet Bately, *The Old English Orosius* published for The Early English Text Society (Supplementary Series 6) 1980. We are grateful to the EETS for permission to adapt our text from this edition.

One page of the manuscript British Library MS Add. 47967 *containing the conclusion of the geography of northern Europe and the beginning of Ohthere's account. Reproduced from* The Tollemache Orosius, *ed. A. Campbell, Copenhagen 1953, by permission of the publishers, Rosenkilde and Bagger.*

cpiraland · be eafian mapeapulonde ipppe lond · þe
eafran þam piirc daru fube lu papon þotan be nopþan
irfran mapoapa pinden dala mthic ran ⁊ be eafrandula
mthic ran pinden honizra ⁊ be nopþan dala mthic ran pin
don rurpe ⁊ bþirfrum him pyple benopþan honera ir maz
þaland ⁊ benopþan mazþalonde rhi mthide oþþa bropzar
piffen · beþirtan rufcanu ir þar zunpterr eapim þelib rmb
utan þer land þmæcannia · ⁊ benopþan him ir þar ror eart
þmen hær ofc pe ⁊ be eafran him ⁊ benopþun pindon nopþ
dthe æþth zeonþæm mapanlandu zeon þam izlandum ⁊
be eafran him pindon afdnede ⁊ beþuþan hi ir ælfe maþa
þahe re ⁊ euldpeacna pimdæl · nopþdthe habbaþ benopþan
him þone ilean rær eapim þænon hær ofc pe ⁊ be eafrun
him pindon ofrj þalfode ⁊ arpede beþuþan ofrj habbaþ
benoþan him þone ilean rær eapim pinedar ⁊ burzen
rarj ⁊ beþuþan him pindon hæ feldun · burzfriðan habbaþ
þone rær eapim beþeyran him ⁊ þrrn benopþun · be eafran
him piirc rþi mthide ⁊ beþuþan him rurre · þþrrn habbaþ
beþuþan him þone rær eapim ofrj ⁊ be eafran him rþimþride
⁊ benopþan him æþenþaþeyrhtne irþrþnland · · beþirfran non
þan him pindon þeynde þinne · ⁊ be þþiran nopþmthin ·

Hic incipit iter plus Ohtheri ·

ctththe ræde hir hlaporde ælfpede cminze þæt he ealpa
nopþ monna nopþ mirc bude · hur ted fær he bude
on þæm lande nopþ peardu piffu rire pre · he ræde
feahþæt lund pre þrifelunz nopþ þonun · uelire ir eal
rþoe buton on reapu ropum frree malu picuð fin
ur on hurrode on purrru ⁊ on rumthu on firrafe
be þthe pæ he ræde þat he æt rumum cmie rolde
fundium hulonze fær lund nopþ ipirxelaze oþþe
hpæðch ænz mon be nopþun þam rtrrrnne bude
þapthe nopþ prhrre beþim lande lælmm ealner

Orosius

Nu wille we ymbe Europe londgemære areccean swa micel swa we hit fyrmest witon.

From þære ie Danais west oþ Rin þa ea, seo wilð of þæm beorge þe mon Alpis hætt & irnð þonne norþryhte on þæs garsecges earm þe þæt lond uton ymblið þe mon Bryttania hætt, & eft suþ oð Donua þa ea, þære æwielme is neah Rines ofre þære ie, & is siþþan east irnende wið norþan Creca lond ut on þone Wendelsæ, & norþ oþ þone garsecg þe mon Cwensæ hæt: binnan þæm sindon monega þeoda, ac hit mon hætt eall Germania.

Þonne wið norþan Donua æwielme & be eastan Rine sindon Eastfrancan, & be suþan him sindon Swæfas, on oþre healfe þære ie Donua, & be suþan him & be eastan sindon Bægware, se dæl þe mon Regnesburg hætt, & ryhte be eastan him sindon Bæme, & east-norþ sindon Þyringas, & be norþan him sindon Ealdseaxan, & be norþanwestan him sindon Frisan. Be westan Ealdseaxum is Ælfe muþa þære ie & Frisland, & þonan westnorð is þæt lond þe mon Ongle hæt & Sillende & sumne dæl Dene, & be norþan him is Af-

Now we intend to record the boundaries within Europe as far as we know them. From the river Don west to the river Rhine (which has its source in the mountains called the Alps, and runs due north into the arm of the ocean surrounding the land called Britain), and also south to the river Danube (the source of which is near the bank of the river Rhine, from where it runs east, north of Greece out into the Mediterranean), and north to the ocean called the *Cwensæ;* within these boundaries are many tribes but it is all called *Germania.*

Then to the north of the Danube's source and to the east of the Rhine are the East Franks, and to the south of them are the *Swæfas* on the other side of the river Danube, and to the south and east of them are the *Bægware* – the part called Regensburg – and directly east of them are the *Bæme* and northeast are the *Thyringas.* To the north of them are the Old Saxons and northwest of them the Frisians. West of the Old Saxons is the mouth of the river Elbe and *Frisland,* and northwest from there is the land which is called Angeln and *Sillende* and some Danish territories. North of them are the *Afdrede* and northeast the *Wilte* known as the *Hæfeldan;* east of them is the

16

drede & eastnorþ Wilte þe mon Hæfeldan hætt, & be eastan him is Wineda lond þe mon hætt Sysyle, & eastsuþ, ofer sumdæl, Maroara; & hie Maroara habbað be westan him þyringas & Behemas & Begware healfe, & be suþan him on oþre healfe Donua þære ie is þæt land Carendre suþ oþ þa beorgas þe mon Alpis hæt; to þæm ilcan beorgan licgað Begwara landgemæro & Swæfa. þonne be eastan Carendran londe, begeondan þæm westenne, is Pulgara land, & be eastan þæm is Creca land, & be eastan Maroara londe is Wisle lond, & be eastan þæm sint Datia, þa þe iu wæron Gotan. Be norþaneastan Maroara sindon Dalamentsan, & be eastan Dalamentsan sindon Horigti, & be norþan Dalamentsan sindon Surpe, & be westan him Sysyle. Be norþan Horoti is Mægþa land, & be norþan Mægþa londe Sermende oþ þa beorgas Riffen. Be westan Suþdenum is þæs garsecges earm þe liþ ymbutan þæt land Brettannia, & be norþan him is þæs sæs earm þe mon hæt Ostsæ, & be eastan him & be norþan sindon Norðdene, ægþer ge on þæm maran landum ge on þæm iglandum, & be eastan him sindon Afdrede, & be suþan him is Ælfe muþa þære ie & Ealdseaxna sumdæl. Norðdene habbað be norþan him þone ilcan sæs earm þe mon hæt Ostsæ, & be eastan him sindon Osti þa leode, & Afdrede be suþan. Osti habbað be norþan him þone ilcan sæs earm & Winedas & Burgendan, & be suþan him sindon Hæfeldan. Burgendan

land of those Wends who are called *Sysyle*, and southeast the *Maroara* who extend over a wide territory; the *Maroara* have to the west of them the *Thyringas* and some *Behemas* and half the *Begware*, and south of them on the other side of the Danube river is the land *Carendre* extending south as far as the mountains called the Alps. To that same mountain range lie the boundaries of the *Begware* and *Swæfas*. Then to the east of the land *Carendre* beyond the uninhabited district is the land of the *Pulgare* and east of that is the land of the Greeks. To the east of the land of the *Maroara* is the land of the Vistula, and east of that are those *Datia* who were formerly Goths. To the north east of the *Maroara* are the *Dalamentsan* and to the east of the *Dalamentsan* are the *Horigti*. North of the *Dalamentsan* are the *Surpe* and west of them the *Sysyle*. To the north of the *Horigti* is *Mægtha* land and to the north of *Mægtha* land the *Sermende* as far as the *Riffen* mountains. West of the South-Danes is the arm of the ocean surrounding Britain, and north of them is the arm of the sea called *Ostsæ*. To the east and north of them are the North-Danes both on the main lands and on the islands. To the east of them are the *Afdrede*, and south of them is the mouth of the river Elbe and part of the Old Saxon lands. The North-Danes have to their north the same arm of the sea which is called the *Ostsæ*, east of them are the tribe the *Osti*, and to the south the *Afdrede*. The *Osti* have to the north of them the same arm of the sea and the Wends and the *Burgendan*; south of them are the *Hæfeldan*. The *Burgendan* habbað þone sæs earm be westan him & Sweon be norþan, & be eastan him sint Sermende, & be suþan him Surfe. Sweon habbað be suþan him þone sæs earm Osti & be eastan him Sermende, & be norþan him ofer þa westenne is Cwenland, & be westannorþan him sindon Scridefinne & be westan Norþmenn.

Ohthere sæde his hlaforde, Ælfrede cyninge, þæt he ealra Norðmonna norþmest bude. He cwæð þæt he bude on þæm lande norþweardum wiþ þa Westsæ. He sæde þeah þæt þæt land sie swiþe lang norþ þonan, ac hit is eal weste, buton on feawum stowum styccemælum wiciað Finnas, on huntoðe on wintra & on sumera on fiscaþe be þære sæ.

He sæde þæt he æt sumum cirre wolde fandian hu longe þæt land norþryhte læge, oþþe hwæðer ænig mon be norðan ðæm westenne bude. Þa for he norþryhte be þæm lande; let him ealne weg þæt weste land on ðæt steorbord & þa widsæ on ðæt bæcbord þrie dagas. Þa wæs he swa feor norþ swa þa hwælhuntan firrest faraþ. Þa for he þa giet norþryhte swa feor swa he meahte on þæm oþrum þrim dagum gesiglan. Þa beag þæt land þær eastryhte, oþþe seo sæ in on ðæt lond, he nysse hwæðer, buton he wisse ðæt he ðær bad westanwindes & hwon norþan &

have the arm of that sea to their west and Swedes to the north. East of them are the *Sermende* and to their south the *Surfe*. The Swedes have south of them the arm of the *Ostsæ* and to their east the *Sermende* and to their north beyond the uninhabited land is *Cwenland*. Northwest of them are the *Scridefinne* and west are the Norwegians.

Ohthere's Account

Ohthere told his lord, King Alfred, that he lived the furthest north of all Norwegians. He said that he lived in the north of Norway on the coast of the Atlantic. He also said that the land extends very far north beyond that point, but it is all uninhabited, except for a few places here and there where the *Finnas* have their camps, hunting in winter, and in summer fishing in the sea.

He told how he once wished to find out how far the land extended due north, or whether anyone lived to the north of the unpopulated area. He went due north along the coast, keeping the uninhabited land to starboard and the open sea to port continuously for three days. He was then as far north as the whale hunters go at their furthest. He then continued due north as far as he could reach in the second three days. There the land turned due east, or the sea penetrated the land he did not know which – but he knew that he waited there for a west-north-west wind, and then sailed east along the coast as far as he could sail in four siglde ða east be lande swa swa he meahte on feower dagum gesiglan. Þa sceolde he ðær bidan ryhtnorþanwindes, for ðæm þæt land beag þær suþryhte, oþþe seo sæ in on ðæt land, he nysse hwæþer. Þa siglde he þonan suðryhte be lande swa swa he mehte on fif dagum gesiglan. Ða læg þær an micel ea up in on þæt land. Þa cirdon hie up in on ða ea, for þæm hie ne dorston forþ bi þære ea siglan for unfriþe, for þæm ðæt land wæs eall gebun on oþre healfe þære eas. Ne mette he ær nan gebun land siþþan he from his agnum ham for, ac him wæs ealne weg weste land on þæt steorbord, butan fiscerum & fugelerum & huntum & þæt wæron eall Finnas, & him wæs a widsæ on ðæt bæcbord. Þa Beormas hæfdon swiþe wel gebud hira land, ac hie ne dorston þæron cuman. Ac þara Terfinna land wæs eal weste, buton ðær huntan gewicodon, oþþe fisceras, oþþe fugeleras.

Fela spella him sædon þa Beormas ægþer ge of hiera agnum lande ge of þæm landum þe ymb hie utan wæron, ac he nyste hwæt þæs soþes wæs, for þæm he hit self ne geseah. Þa Finnas, him þuhte, & þa Beormas spræcon neah an geþeode. Swiþost he for ðider, toeacan þæs landes sceawunge, for þæm horshwælum, for ðæm hie habbað

days. There he had to wait for a due northern wind, because there the land turned due south, or the sea penetrated the land he did not know which. Then from there he sailed due south along the coast as far as he could sail in five days. A great river went up into the land there. They turned up into the river, not daring to sail beyond it without permission, since the land on the far side of the river was fully settled. He had not previously come across any settled district since he left his own home, but had, the whole way, land to starboard that was uninhabited apart from fishers and bird-catchers and hunters, and they were all *Finnas*. To port he always had the open sea. The *Beormas* had extensive settlements in their country but the Norwegians did not dare to venture there. But the land of the *Terfinnas* was totally uninhabited except where hunters made camp, or fishermen or bird-catchers.

The *Beormas* told him many stories both about their own country and about the lands which surrounded them, but he did not know how much of it was true because he had not seen it for himself. It seemed to him that the *Finnas* and the *Beormas* spoke almost the same language. His main reason for going there, apart from exploring the land, was for the walruses, because they have

swiþe æþele ban on hiora toþum – þa teð hie
brohton sume þæm cyninge – & hiora hyd
bið swiðe god to sciprapum. Se hwæl bið
micle læssa þonne oðre hwalas: ne bið he
lengra ðonne syfan elna lang; ac on his
agnum lande is se betsta hwælhuntað: þa
beoð eahta and feowertiges elna lange, & þa
mæstan fiftiges elna lange; þara he sæde þæt
he syxa sum ofsloge syxtig on twam dagum.

He wæs swyðe spedig man on þæm æhtum
þe heora speda on beoð, þæt is on wildrum.
He hæfde þagyt, ða he þone cyningc sohte,
tamra deora unbebohtra syx hund. þa deor
hi hatað hranas; þara wæron syx stælhranas,
ða beoð swyðe dyre mid Finnum, for ðæm hy
foð þa wildan hranas mid. He wæs mid þæm
fyrstum mannum on þæm lande; næfde he
þeah ma ðonne twentig hryðera & twentig
sceapa & twentig swyna, & þæt lytle þæt he
erede he erede mid horsan. Ac hyra ar is
mæst on þæm gafole þe ða Finnas him
gyldað. Þæt gafol bið on deora fellum & on
fugela feðerum & hwales bane & on þæm
sciprapum þe beoð of hwæles hyde geworht
& of seoles. Æghwilc gylt be hys gebyrdum:
se byrdesta sceall gyldan fiftyne mearðes fell
& fif hranes & an beran fel & tyn ambra
feðra & berenne kyrtel oððe yterenne &
twegen sciprapas; ægþer sy syxtig elna lang:
oþer sy of hwæles hyde geworht, oþer of
sioles.

He sæde ðæt Norðmanna land wære swyþe
lang & swyðe smæl. Eal þæt his man aþer

very fine ivory in their tusks – they brought some
of these tusks to the king – and their hide is very
good for ship-ropes. This whale [i.e. walrus] is
much smaller than other whales; it is no more
than seven ells long. The best whale-hunting is in
his own country; those are forty-eight ells long,
the biggest fifty ells long; of these he said that he,
one of six, killed sixty in two days.

He was a very rich man in those possessions
which their riches consist of, that is in wild deer.
He had still, when he came to see the king, six
hundred unsold tame deer. These deer they call
'reindeer'. Six of these were decoy-reindeer.
These are very valuable among the *Finnas*
because they use them to catch the wild reindeer.
He was among the chief men in that country, but
he had not more than twenty cattle, twenty sheep
and twenty pigs, and the little that he ploughed
he ploughed with horses. Their wealth, however,
is mostly in the tribute which the *Finnas* pay
them. That tribute consists of the skins of beasts,
the feathers of birds, whale-bone, and ship-ropes
made from whale-hide and sealskin. Each pays
according to his rank. The highest in rank has to
pay fifteen marten skins, five reindeer skins, one
bear skin and ten measures of feathers, and a
jacket of bearskin or otterskin and two ship-
ropes. Each of these must be sixty ells long, one
made from whale-hide the other from seal.

He said that the land of the Norwegians is very
long and narrow. All of it that can be used for
grazing or ploughing lies along the coast and even
that is in some places very rocky. Wild mountains

oððe ettan oððe erian mæg, þæt lið wið ða sæ; & þæt is þeah on sumum stowum swyðe cludig, & licgað wilde moras wið eastan & wið uppon, emnlange þæm bynum lande. On þæm morum eardiað Finnas: & þæt byne land is easteweard bradost & symle swa norðor swa smælre; eastewerd hit mæg bion syxtig mila brad oþþe hwene brædre, & middeweard þritig oððe bradre; & norðe-weard, he cwæð, þær hit smalost wære, þæt hit mihte beon þreora mila brad to þæm more, & se mor syðþan on sumum stowum swa brad swa man mæg on twam wucum oferferan, & on sumum stowum swa brad swa man mæg on syx dagum oferferan. Ðonne is toemnes þæm lande suðeweardum, on oðre healfe þæs mores, Sweoland, oþ þæt land norðeweard; & toemnes þæm lande norðeweardum Cwena land. þa Cwenas hergiað hwilum on ða Norðmen ofer ðone mor, hwilum þa Norðmen on hy, & þær sint swiðe micle meras fersce geond þa moras, & beraþ þa Cwenas hyra scypu ofer land on ða meras & þanon hergiað on ða Norðmen; hy habbað swyðe lytle scypa & swyðe leohte.

Ohthere sæde þæt sio scir hatte Halgoland þe he on bude. He cwæð þæt nan man ne bude be norðan him. þonne is an port on suðeweardum þæm lande þone man hæt Sciringesheal. þyder he cwæð þæt man ne mihte geseglian on anum monðe, gyf man on niht wicode & ælce dæge hæfde ambyrne

lie to the east, above and alongside the cultivated land. In these mountains live the *Finnas*. The cultivated land is broadest in the south, and the further north it goes the narrower it becomes. In the south it is perhaps sixty miles broad or a little broader; and in the middle, thirty or broader; and to the north, he said, where it is narrowest, it might be three miles across to the mountains. The mountains beyond are in some places of a width that takes two weeks to cross, in others of a width that can be crossed in six days.

Beyond the mountains Sweden borders the southern part of the land as far as the north, and the country of the *Cwenas* borders the land in the north. Sometimes the *Cwenas* make raids on the Norwegians across the mountains, and sometimes the Norwegians make raids on them. There are very large fresh-water lakes throughout these mountains, and the *Cwenas* carry their boats overland onto the lakes and from there make raids on the Norwegians. They have very small, very light boats.

Ohthere said that the district where he lived is called *Halgoland*. He said no-one lived to the north of him. In the south part of Norway there is a trading-town which is called *Sciringes heal*. He said that a man could scarcely sail there in a month, assuming he made camp at night, and each day had a favourable wind. He would sail by the coast the whole way. To starboard is first of all *Iraland* and then those islands which are between *Iraland* and this land, and then this land until he comes to *Sciringes heal*, and Norway is on the port wind; & ealle ða hwile he sceal seglian be lande; & on þæt steorbord him bið ærest Iraland, & þonne ða igland þe synd betux Iralande & þissum lande; þonne is þis land oð he cymð to Scirincgesheale, & ealne weg on þæt bæcbord Norðweg. Wið suðan þone Sciringesheal fylð swyðe mycel sæ up in on ðæt land, seo is bradre þonne ænig man ofer seon mæge, & is Gotland on oðre healfe ongean & siððan Sillende. Seo sæ lið mænig hund mila up in on þæt land: & of Sciringesheale he cwæð þæt he seglode on fif dagan to þæm porte þe mon hæt æt Hæþum, se stent betuh Winedum & Seaxum & Angle & hyrð in on Dene. Ða he þiderweard seglode fram Sciringesheale, þa wæs him on þæt bæcbord Denamearc & on þæt steorbord widsæ þry dagas; & þa, twegen dagas ær he to Hæþum come, him wæs on þæt steorbord Gotland & Sillende & iglanda fela – on þæm landum eardodon Engle, ær hi hider on land coman – & hym wæs ða twegen dagas on ðæt bæcbord þa igland þe in Denemearce hyrað.

Wulfstan sæde þæt he gefore of Hæðum, þæt he wære on Truso on syfan dagum & nihtum, þæt þæt scip wæs ealne weg yrnende under segle. Weonoðland him wæs on steorbord & on bæcbord him wæs Langaland & Læland & Falster & Sconeg, & þas land eall hyrað to Denemearcan: & þonne Burgenda land wæs us on bæcbord, & þa habbað him sylf cyning. Þonne æfter Burgenda lande

side the whole way. To the south of *Sciringes heal* a great sea penetrates the land; it is too wide to see across. Jutland is on the far side and after that *Sillende*. This sea flows into the land for many hundred miles.

From *Sciringes heal* he said that he sailed in five days to the trading-town called Hedeby, which is situated among Wends, Saxons and Angles and belongs to the Danes. When he sailed there from *Sciringes heal* he had Denmark to port and the open sea to starboard for three days. Then two days before he arrived at Hedeby he had Jutland and *Sillende* and many islands to starboard. The Angles lived in these districts before they came to this land. On the port side he had, for two days, those islands which belong to Denmark.

Wulfstan's Account

Wulfstan said that he travelled from Hedeby, arriving in Truso after seven days and nights, the boat running under sail the whole way. To starboard he had Wendland, to port Langeland, Lolland, Falster and Skåne. All these lands belong to Denmark.

wæron us þas land þa synd hatene ærest
Blecingaeg & Meore & Eowland & Gotland
on bæcbord, & þas land hyrað to Sweon: &
Weonodland wæs us ealne weg on steorbord
oð Wislemuðan. Seo Wisle is swyðe mycel ea
& hio tolið Witland & Weonodland, & þæt
Witland belimpeð to Estum, & seo Wisle lið
ut of Weonodlande & lið in Estmere, & se
Estmere is huru fiftene mila brad; þonne
cymeð Ilfing eastan in Estmere of ðæm mere
ðe Truso standeð in staðe, & cumað ut samod
in Estmere, Ilfing eastan of Estlande & Wisle
suðan of Winodlande; & þonne benimð
Wisle Ilfing hire naman & ligeð of þæm
mere west & norð on sæ: for ðy hit man hæt
Wislemuða.

Þæt Estland is swyðe mycel, & þær bið
swyðe manig burh, & on ælcere byrig bið
cyningc, & þær bið swyðe mycel hunig &
fiscað, & se cyning & þa ricostan men drincað
myran meolc, & þa unspedigan & þa þeowan
drincað medo. Þær bið swyðe mycel gewinn
betweonan him: & ne bið ðær nænig ealo
gebrowen mid Estum, ac þær bið medo
genoh: & þær is mid Estum ðeaw, þonne þær
bið man dead, þæt he lið inne unforbærned
mid his magum & freondum monað ge
hwilum twegen, & þa kyningas & þa oðre
heahðungene men swa micle lencg swa hi
maran speda habbað, hwilum healf gear þæt
hi beoð unforbærned & licgað bufan eorðan
on hyra husum: & ealle þa hwile þe þæt lic
bið inne, þær sceal beon gedrync & plega, oð

'Then we had Bornholm to port, where the
people have their own king. Then after Bornholm
we had on our port side the lands which are called
Blekinge, Möre, Øland and Gotland, and these
lands belong to the Swedes. Wendland was to
starboard the whole of the way to the mouth of
the Vistula.' This Vistula is a very large river
which separates Witland and Wendland. Witland
belongs to the *Este*. The Vistula flows out of
Wendland into Estmere which is at least fifteen
miles wide. The Elbing flows into Estmere from
the lake on the shore of which Truso stands, and
they flow together into Estmere, the Elbing west
from Estland and the Vistula north from Wendland. Then the Vistula deprives the Elbing of its
name – for the estuary is known as the Vistula
estuary – and flows from Estmere northwest into
the sea.

This Estland is very large and has many
fortified settlements, and in each of these there is
a king. There is a great deal of honey and fishing.
The king and the most powerful men drink
mare's milk, the poor men and the slaves drink
mead. There is very much strife among them.
There is no ale brewed among the *Este* but there
is plenty of mead. There is a custom among the
Este that after a man's death he lies indoors
uncremated among his relatives and friends for a
month, sometimes two. The kings and other
high-ranking men remain uncremated sometimes
for half a year – the more wealth they have the
longer they lie above ground in their houses. All
the time that the corpse lies indoors it is the

ðone dæg þe hi hine forbærnað. þonne þy ylcan dæg þe hi hine to þæm ade beran wyllað, þonne todælað hi his feoh, þæt þær to lafe bið æfter þæm gedrynce & þæm plegan, on fif oððe syx, hwylum on ma, swa swa þæs feos andefn bið. Alecgað hit ðonne forhwæga on anre mile þone mæstan dæl fram þæm tune, þonne oðerne, ðonne þæne þriddan, oþ þe hyt eall aled bið on þære anre mile; & sceall beon se læsta dæl nyhst þæm tune ðe se deada man on lið. Ðonne sceolon beon gesamnode ealle ða menn ðe swyftoste hors habbað on þæm lande, forhwæga on fif milum oððe on syx milum fram þæm feo. Þonne ærnað hy ealle toweard þæm feo; ðonne cymeð se man se þæt swiftoste hors hafað to þæm ærestan dæle & to þæm mæstan, & swa ælc æfter oðrum, oþ hit bið eall genumen; & se nimð þone læstan dæl se nyhst þæm tune þæt feoh geærneð: & þonne rideð ælc hys weges mid ðan feo & hyt motan habban eall, & for ðy þær beoð þa swiftan hors ungefoge dyre: & þonne hys gestreon beoð þus eall aspended, þonne byrð man hine ut & forbærneð mid his wæpnum & hrægle, & swiðost ealle hys speda hy forspendað mid þan langan legere þæs deadan mannes inne & þæs þe hy be þæm wegum alecgað, þe ða fremdan to ærnað & nimað: & þæt is mid Estum þeaw þæt þær sceal ælces geðeodes man beon forbærned, & gyf þar man an ban findeð unforbærned, hi hit sceolan miclum gebetan: & þær is mid Estum an mægð þæt hi magon

custom for there to be drinking and gambling until the day on which they cremate it. On the very day on which they intend to carry the dead man to the pyre, they divide his property – whatever is left of it after the drinking and gambling – into five or six portions, sometimes more, depending on how much there is. They place the biggest portion about a mile from the settlement, then the second, then the third, until it is all distributed within the mile, so that the smallest portion is closest to the place where the dead man lies. All the men who have the swiftest horses in the country are assembled at a point about five or six miles from the property, and then they all gallop towards it. The man who has the fastest horse comes to the first portion (which is also the largest) and then one after another until it has all been taken. He has the smallest portion who gets from his ride the one nearest to the settlement. Then each of them rides on his way with the property and is allowed to keep it all. For this reason good horses are extremely valuable there. When the man's treasures have all been spent in this way, then he is carried out and burned up with his weapons and clothes. They use up most of the dead man's wealth with what they squander during the long period of his lying in the house, and with what they put by the wayside which strangers ride up to and take. It is the custom among the *Este* that the men of each tribe are cremated, and if one bone is found not completely burned, heavy compensation must be paid.

cyle gewyrcan, & þy þær licgað þa deadan men swa lange & ne fuliað, þæt hy wyrcað þone cyle hine on, & þeah man asette twegen fætels full ealað oððe wæteres, hy gedoð þæt oþer bið oferfroren, sam hit sy sumor, sam winter.

There is a tribe among the *Este* that knows how to cause cold, and this is why the dead men there lie so long and do not rot, because they keep them cold. If two containers are put out full of beer or water, they can cause one of the two to be frozen over whether it is summer or winter.

'Saga Siglar', replica of Skuldelev 1, a deep-sea ship, coming through Øresund in August 1983. Photo: Vikingeskibs-hallen, Roskilde, Denmark.

WESTSÆ
(ATLANTIC OCEAN)

(SCRIDE) FINNAS

SEE P. 65

HALGOLAND

CWENLAND

NORÐWEG

SWEON

SCIRINGESHEAL
(KAUPANG)

UPPLAND

BIRKA

VÄSTER
GÖTLAND

ÖSTER
GÖTLAND

HALLAND

SMÅLAND

MÉORE

GOTLAND

EOWLAND

GOTLAND

BLECINGAEG

SCONEG

RIBE

WISLE

SILLENDE

NIEMEN

ÆT HÆÞUM
(HEDEBY)

ONGLE

BURGENDA
LAND

OSTI

AFDREDE
HAMBURG

TRUSO

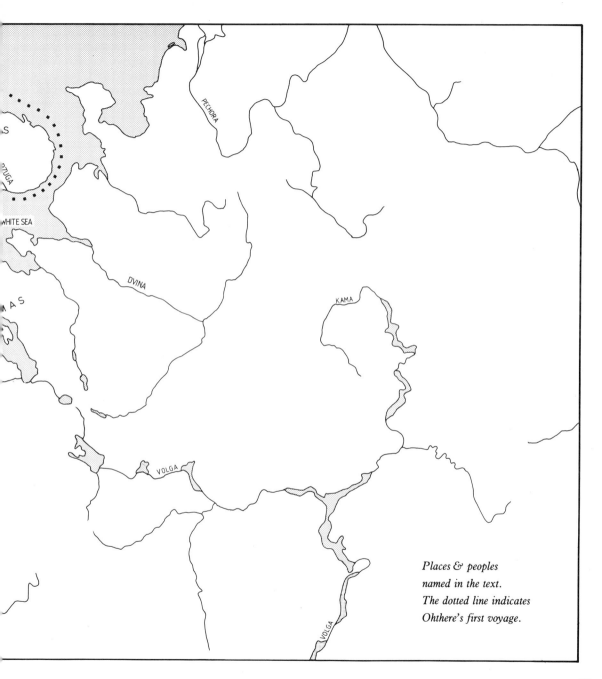

PECHORA

WHITE SEA

DVINA

KAMA

VOLGA

VOLGA

Places & peoples
named in the text.
The dotted line indicates
Ohthere's first voyage.

KIEV

VOLGA

DANAIS

*Places & peoples
named in the text.*

Ships, navigation and routes in the reports of Ohthere and Wulfstan

OLE CRUMLIN-PEDERSEN

Unlike many other accounts of early voyages, Ohthere's journey along the western and northern edges of Scandinavia and the Kola peninsula can easily be traced on a modern map. The goods that this north Norwegian chieftain was able to take to the markets of south Scandinavia included not only his own produce and the tribute that he gathered from the Lapps in his area but also some wares that had come from the inner reaches of the White Sea. As for his journey to England, we may assume that he sailed there directly with his goods and made his way to Alfred's court partly in order to offer gifts to the king who was the protector of trade. This route between Norway and England was, however, so well known that it was not worth giving a detailed description of it.

The normal route for Ohthere's trading journeys was clearly along the Norwegian coast to *Sciringesheal*. He described this voyage in very general terms as taking more than a month if the winds were favourable and with no sailing at night. The distance along the coast from Ohthere's home in Halogaland to *Sciringesheal* is about 1750 km or 950 nautical miles and if we assume it took 30 days each of 16 hours the average speed was 2 knots. His journeys to Hedeby and the White Sea, on the other hand,

seem to have been occasional, not regular, and only the outward voyages are described. This enabled him to report his best sailing times, rather as modern yachtsmen would prefer to talk about their fastest passages than those on which they were forced to lie waiting for a favourable wind. This must be borne in mind when tracing Ohthere's route from *Sciringesheal* to Hedeby. The following attempt to do this is based not only on the information he himself gave, but also on our current knowledge of sailing in the Viking period.

The route has often been discussed, generally in connection with learned discussions about the interpretation of the regional names (*Denamearc, Gotland, Sillende*) mentioned by Ohthere. Here we will go a step further and also take into account what is known about contemporary sailing techniques, natural harbours and the physical constraints that affect anyone who sails along the possible routes through Danish waters. We will begin by accepting the interpretations of the names that now seem to be generally agreed, that is: *Denamearc* = Denmark meaning the areas that were apparently under Danish rule, Sjælland, Skåne, Halland and possibly Bohuslän. *Gotland* = (North) Jutland as far south as the area

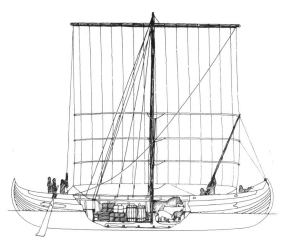

Skuldelev 1, deep-sea ship (16.3 m long and 4.5 m broad) excavated in Roskilde fjord 1962. Reconstruction by Erik Andersen and Ole Crumlin-Pedersen, Vikingeskibshallen, Roskilde, Denmark.

around Kolding, and *Sillende* = South Jutland as far south as Hedeby, possibly excluding the west coast. It is not clear in which of these three 'lands' Ohthere reckoned Fyn to lie, and after traversing the west coast of Sweden and the north coast of Sjælland, he could therefore have gone through either Store Bælt or Lille Bælt (see map).

Before considering the route in detail something should be said about Ohthere's ship and its sailing characteristics. The Gokstad and Oseberg ships were of about the same period but they were *karfar* (sg. *karfi*) and their main purpose was to carry men and their equipment. Ohthere's vessel was hardly of that type. He is more likely to have sailed a large cargo-boat, probably a type of *knarr* related to, but over a century older than, the ship

known as Skuldelev 1. The existence of specialised cargo-boats before the year 900 is demonstrated by two somewhat neglected ships of the early Viking period; the Klåstad ship, found only 6 km from *Sciringesheal* with the remains of a load of whetstones and dated to about 800, and the Äskekärr boat, discovered in the banks of Göta Älv and dated to the ninth or tenth century. These ships were 14-16 m long and capacious, with half decks fore and aft leaving an open cargo hold amidships, as in the cargo-boats found at Skuldelev.

The wood used in the construction of these ships can help to determine where they were built. Thus the Gokstad, Oseberg, Klåstad and Äskekärr ships were all made mainly, or entirely,

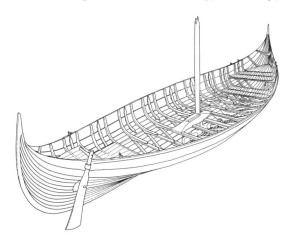

The Klåstad merchant ship (21 m long and 5 m broad) from c. AD 800, found near Kaupang. Reconstruction by Arne Emil Christensen and Gunnar Leiro, Universitetets Oldsaksamling, Oslo.

of oak while Skuldelev 1 is largely pine. This suggests that while Skuldelev 1 was made somewhere along the west coast of Norway, the others were from the Skagerrak-Kattegat region where oaks grew. If, as seems likely, Ohthere's ship was built in west Norway it was very likely the same type as Skuldelev 1, but without that ship's very strong ribs which are, in fact, larger than any other Viking ship. Skuldelev 1 was 16.3 m long and 4.5 m broad. With a load of 15-20 tons it drew about 1.5 m and the sail area may be estimated as about 100 m². With such a ship Ohthere would have been able to carry a sufficiently large cargo of both heavy goods (soap-stone and whetstones) as well as lighter things (furs, skins, ropes, walrus tusks) to make a very good profit with a single annual voyage.

The description of Ohthere's personal status suggests that he himself probably owned both ship and cargo, and that the crew, probably eight to ten, were his own men. Some other trading enterprises were probably joint enterprises by a small group of travelling merchants, each owning a part of the cargo and trading individually but all sharing the work of handling the ship.

On several occasions during his voyage to the White Sea, when the general direction of the coast changed, Ohthere waited for a following wind. It would however be wrong to conclude that his ship was unable to sail close to the wind. The explanation is, rather, that on entering unknown waters, Ohthere wanted as much wind-room as possible for manoeuvres so that he

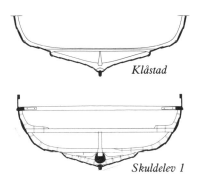

Klåstad

Skuldelev 1

could without difficulty avoid any unexpected obstacles that might occur. Had he attempted to reach, that is sail with the wind abeam, or to sail on the wind in waters with complex currents and with the possibility of snow showers, there was a risk that he might not be able to sail out of danger. The lines of the hull and details of the rigging of Viking ships that have so far been found show that at least the cargo-boats were designed to have a good capacity to tack against the wind. Experiments with replicas of Viking ships and with related modern boats with square sails have shown that such a cargo-boat could have been sailed as close as about five points (55°-60°) to the wind and could, by tacking, make in effect 1.5 to 2.0 knots against the direction of the wind. In narrow waters, however, where the current often runs in the same direction as the wind blows, a ship can easily meet an opposing current too strong to be overcome against a contrary wind. In such circumstances, in the Viking period as at all other times in the history of sailing, it was necessary to anchor to wait for a wind that was more favourable in terms of either strength or direction, or both. The ideal conditions for a Viking ship were to have the wind abeam or on a stern quarter, and with a speed of 6-12 m/second (11-22 knots). To judge by the analyses and experiments so far made, Viking period cargo-boats could, under ideal conditions, maintain an average speed of 6 to 8 knots during a day's sailing, with a probable maximum of up to 10-12 knots in a strong breeze (10-12 m/second, 18-36 knots).

Voyages are, however, normally not made in ideal conditions and, as we have seen, the long trip from Halogaland to *Sciringesheal* took at least a whole month at an average speed of 2 knots. Ohthere explicitly stated that the voyage was interrupted every night, the ship presumably being either anchored or beached. This method of coastal sailing was probably the one most commonly adopted in the Viking period, making it possible to travel without compass or other navigational aids, other than a local pilot familiar with dangerous skerries, land marks and natural harbours along the route. Even in the thirteenth century this was a favoured method of sailing in the Baltic, as is shown by an account of the route from Blekinge to Estonia that is incorporated in King Valdemar's *Jordebog* (Land Survey). This carefully describes a coastal route up to the Stockholm archipelago, through the Åland islands, and along the coast of south Finland, instead of the direct route across the sea via Öland, Gotland and Ösel. A similar method of navigation was appropriate for the coasts of Norway and western Sweden, with their skerries, or in Danish waters where there are many fjords, creeks and bays in which a ship can shelter in hours of darkness, while in the daytime it was possible to sail well outside the dangerous reefs and banks.

We can now, in the light of these considerations, attempt to trace the most likely route from *Sciringesheal* to Hedeby. Ohthere first sailed for three days along the coast of *Denamearc* with the open sea to starboard, and the next two days he had islands that belonged to Denamearc to port and *Gotland, Sillende* and many islands to starboard. The total length of the route is about 375 nautical miles through Store Bælt and 400 through Lille Bælt, meaning an average of 75-80 miles a day, or an average speed of five knots with 16 hours sailing a day. Such a high average speed means that the wind must have blown fairly strongly and steadily from NW, N or NE so that Ohthere had no need to tack. In such conditions we are justified in attempting to determine the stages of the journey on the assumption that his ship did in fact maintain a fairly constant daily rate of about 80 miles for the five days.

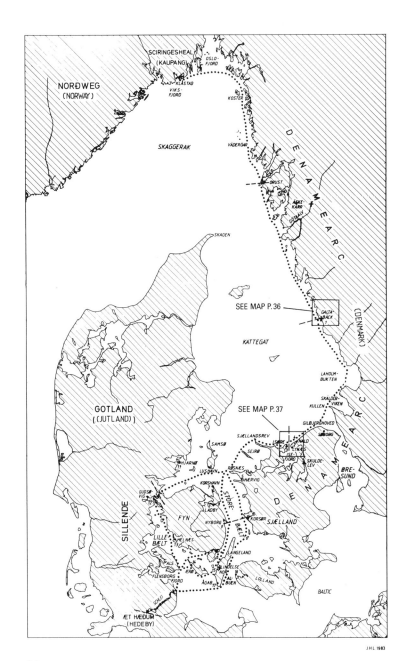

NORÐWEG
(NORWAY)

SCIRINGESHEAL
(KAUPANG)

OSLO-
FJORD

KLÅSTAD

VIKS-
FJORD

KOSTER

SKAGGERAK

VADERØR

D
E
N
A
M
E
A
R
C

ORUST

ÅSKE-
KÄRR

GOTHAVN

SKAGEN

SEE MAP P. 36

GALTA-
BÄCK

C(DENMARK)

KATTEGAT

LAHOLM-
BUKTEN

SKALDER-
VIKEN

KULLEN

GILBJERGHOVED

GOTLAND
(JUTLAND)

SEE MAP P. 37

SJÆLLANDSREV

SAMSØ

SEJRØ

SØBORG

ISØRE
ISE-
FJORD

NÆLD

LYNÆS

SKULDE-
LEV

D
E
N
A
M
E
A
R
C

ØRE-
SUND

HJARNØ

LUS HAVN

RØSNÆS

KORSHAVN

SNERVIG

GUDSØ
VIG

LADBY

FYN

NYBORG

S
T
O
R
E
-
B
Æ
L
T

KORSØR

SJÆLLAND

SILLENDE

HELNÆS

LILLE-
BÆLT

LANGELAND

ALS

SNØDE

GULDELSE

AL-
BUEN

LOLLAND

FLENSBORG
FJORD

ERØ

ÅGAB

BALTIC

SLIEI

ÆT HÆÐUM
(HEDEBY)

JHL 1983

Ohthere's route from Kaupang to
Hedeby, with indications of a likely
day's sailing, of good anchorages,
and of various possible passages
through the islands.

Day 1: After leaving Viksfjord they sailed east across the entrance to Oslo Fjord and south along the coast by Koster and the Väderöar to Orust, where there are countless good overnight anchorages.

Day 2: The journey continued either outside or through the skerries (archipelago) at the mouth of Göta Älv and then SE where the skerries peter out and the coastal waters become shallower. There are, however, bays that can serve as natural havens, for example *Galtabäckslagunen* south of Varberg (no 1 on the map). Two medieval ship-wrecks have been found there. These vessels obviously sank while anchored near a site called *Gamla Köpstad* which is thought to have been Varberg's predecessor as a local trading place. We do not know if a coastal market was already held there in Ohthere's time, or whether Ohthere actually did visit that place after sailing for two days, but it certainly fits very well the distance that he can be reckoned to have travelled.

Day 3: The journey continued past Laholmbukten and Skälderviken to the high promontory of Kullen which is an obvious turning point. From here it is possible to see Gilbjerg Hoved, the northern tip of Sjælland, in clear weather and it is therefore possible to cross the entrance to the Sound at this point without losing sight of land ahead. The route then continues SW along the coast of north Sjælland and by nightfall Ohthere would have been close to the entrance to Isefjord. Here there are several possible places in which to shelter from a northerly wind. Inside the entrance, east of Lynæs is *Skuldevig* (no 2). Here was a coastal market from the eighth to the twelfth century and the remains of two or three ships of the latter part of that period were found here in 1975. On the west side of the fjord's entrance there was another good anchorage at *Isøre* (no 3). This was one of the places at which the *leiðangr* fleet assembled in the eleventh and twelfth centuries and a *þing* was occasionally held there during that period. Another possibility was to run into a bay on the north side of *Halsnæs* (no 4), which is now silted up, and seek shelter in the lee of the little peninsula whose name *Hald* is reminiscent of the sagas' unidentified great market at Haløre.

Day 4: The first stage of this day's sailing was perhaps the most difficult and dangerous of the whole voyage. It was necessary to follow Sjællands Odde W and NW to the point and then some distance beyond in order to cross the reef known as Sjællands Rev. At Snekkeløbet, the narrow passage in the reef, ships often meet churning choppy seas. That hazard past, Ohthere would have sailed for the outer point of first Sejrø and then Røsnæs. A decision then had to be made whether to continue through Store Bælt or Lille Bælt. The latter route is 25 miles longer but if the wind continued to blow from the north, as it had done for several days, Ohthere could expect to have the help of a current through Lille Bælt. The

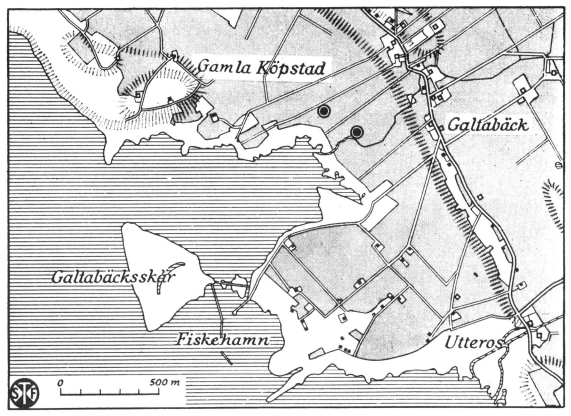

Galtabäck lagoon, Halland, showing where two early medieval wrecks were found at Gamla Köpstad, now waste ground, but probably once Varberg's fore-runner (Humbla 1937).

currents in Store Bælt are more irregular, often flowing in opposite directions in different places at the same time. In such circumstances both routes would probably have taken much the same time.

If shelter were needed after passing Røsnæs there were several good possibilities: *Hærvig* in Kalundborg Fjord (no 5), later one of the main stations of the *leiðangr* fleet; *Lushavn*, a bay that is now silted up on the south shore of Samsø near *Vesborg* (no 6), which may have been one of the two harbours on Samsø mentioned in the sagas; or *Korshavn*, a natural haven at Fyns Hoved (no 7). In Store Bælt itself there were several sheltered anchorages on the coast of Fyn and one of these was at Ladby in the outer part of

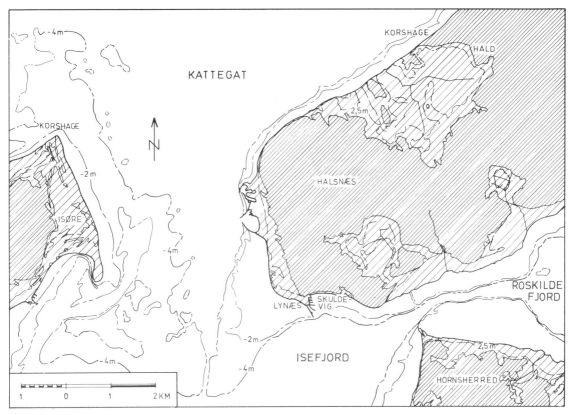

The entrance to Ise fjord and Roskilde fjord. The bays at Isøre and Skuldevig served as natural harbours, as did presumably the creek, now silted up, at Hald on the north side of Halsnæs.

Kerteminde Fjord (no 8). The boat-grave found there and the name itself (*by* at the loading place) both point to maritime activity in the Viking period. There were also secure anchorages in Nyborg Fjord (no 9) and in Korsør Nor (no 10) and we may suppose that Ohthere used one of these if he went that way.

If he went north of Fyn he could have anchored

at Hjarnø in the mouth of Horsens Fjord (no 11). A bay, now silted up, was an ideal natural haven in an island that, significantly, has many stone ship-settings of the Viking period. With a good wind and current Ohthere's fourth day could, however, have taken him as far as the northern part of Lille Bælt. Underwater barriers and a medieval wreck found at *Gudsø Vig* and *Eltang*

Vig (no 12) show that this may have been a maritime centre at the time and Ohthere could have anchored there overnight.

Day 5: In Lille Bælt both wind and current would have helped Ohthere's southerly run. He reported that he had Jutland, *Sillende* and many islands to starboard and if he did indeed go this way he must therefore have sailed along the coast of Fyn so that Brandsø, Bågø, Årø, Barsø and Als ('many islands') were on his starboard side. There were several good anchorages and natural harbours on that route if they were needed, such as *Helnæs* (no 13) where an underwater defensive barrier was constructed across the entrance to the bay in about 1100, or the now dried-up *Vitsø Nor* at the NW end of Ærø (no 14), where in recent years investigations have revealed evidence of maritime activity in the Roman Iron Age and in the Middle Ages (contemporary with the royal fort). From the south end of Als the route to the mouth of the Schlei crossed the entrance to Als Sund and Flensborg Fjord.

In Store Bælt it was possible to sail east or west of Langeland. The most direct route was to the west and on through the archipelago south of Fyn but the navigable channels are narrow and it is likely that even then the passage between Ærø and Langeland was difficult and required intimate local knowledge. Shelter could be had in *Lindelse Nor* (no 15). From the south point of Ærø it is 16 miles to the mouth of the Schlei, that is a good three hours sailing at five knots. If Ohthere chose to go east of Langeland he presumably followed the coast of Sjælland, west of Agersø and Omø, and then the east coast of Langeland which is clear of banks and reefs but offers no shelter. There was, however, a haven at the western point of Lolland at *Albuen* (no 16). A rich herring fishery and market developed in this natural harbour during the Middle Ages. At the southern point of Langeland he could have found sheltered anchorages at *Keldsnor* and *Ågab* (no 17) if the weather did not allow the crossing of the 23 miles to the Schlei. These routes through Store Bælt all required a three to five hours sail to the Schlei partly out of sight of land. This could be avoided by making a detour along the coast of Ærø to Vitsø Nor and from there it is only six miles across Lille Bælt to Als. It was also possible to reach Lille Bælt at a narrow crossing point by sailing through Svendborg Sund instead of following the south coast of Langeland. Finally a 22 mile stretch through the Schlei narrows brought Ohthere and his men to Hedeby and their journey's end.

We do not know whether navigation marks were erected in the Viking period or if there were other attempts to facilitate sailing in northern waters. The construction of the Kanhave canal across Samsø in the second half of the eighth century must be considered a sign of royal interest in the control of sea traffic along the coast of Jutland at that time. Viking traders made payments to the king in order to secure peace in the markets and it was therefore in the interest of

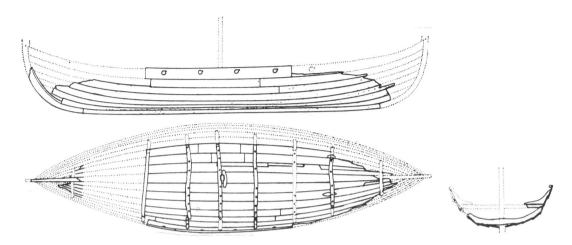

Wendish vessel 9.5 m long. A rowing or sailing boat found during excavations at Ralswiek on Rügen in 1967 (Herfert 1968).

both parties to ensure that journeys could be made without hindrance from pirates, for example. It would therefore not be surprising if one day it proves possible to show archaeologically that one of the important functions of royal power in the Viking period was to help shipping in general.

Wulfstan's journey was obviously very different from Ohthere's, first and foremost because the ship in which he travelled to Truso did not anchor overnight but sailed continuously for seven days. The total distance is about 420 nautical miles and the average speed was therefore about 2.5 knots. This voyage can be divided into daily sections of 60 miles but in this case this calculation has less interest. The wind could have varied greatly in both force and direction during the journey and the ship could, for example, have been becalmed for two days and sailed at 3.5 knots for the rest of the time. Was it an English or Frisian ship that had come through Limfjorden, or Scandinavian or Slav? A cargo-boat or warship? It is perhaps most likely that Wulfstan travelled in one of the Slav cargo-boats that must have sailed along this coast in the Viking period. Remains of a ninth-century example of one have been found sunk at Schuby south of the Schlei mouth.

Here we will attempt to determine the navigation techniques used on this route, which must have been the same for all ships at that time irrespective of provenance or type. Along the south coast of the Baltic the conditions for sailing were entirely different from those along the

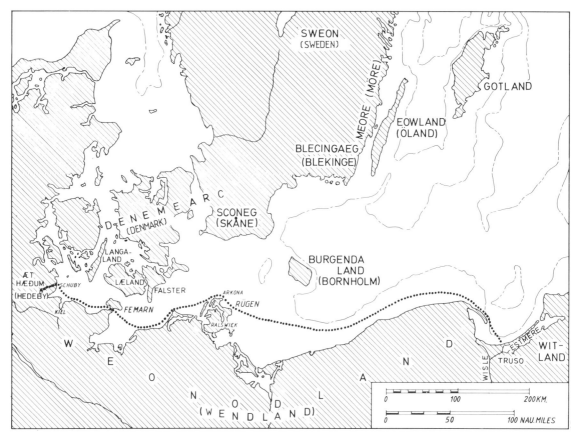

Wulfstan's probable route from Hedeby to Truso.

northern coasts discussed above because of the estuaries of large and small rivers and the shallow beaches. Here most of the small bays and inlets that could have been used as anchorages were probably already then closed by the movement of large quantities of material along this coast. Only around Rügen is the pattern different with deeply indented bays and creeks. The trading place

Ralswiek was there and has yielded many indications of close connections between Rügen and Denmark in the Viking period. Remains of Slav ships showing Scandinavian influence have also been found there.

In order to sail at night as well as in the day along such a coast it was necessary to be able to measure depth with a lead to ensure that a safe

English ship from the Bayeux tapestry with a man casting the lead at work in the bow (Stenton, 1957).

distance was kept from the shore. As indicated on the map, it can be assumed that the ship followed the general line of the coast (for example along the 10 m depth line) past Eckernförde and Kiel Fjord to Femer Sund. From there the route was south-east until the 10 m depth is reached again and that line could be followed as far north as Arkona on the north of Rügen. Thereafter the skipper could choose to follow the 10 m line or, as indicated on the map, the more direct route along the well-defined 20 m depth that leads to the

estuaries of the Vistula (Wisle) and Elbing in Gdansk Bay, and the journey ended with the short crossing of the Estmere to Truso on the bank of the Elbing.

It is obviously difficult to prove archaeologically that depth-sounding with a lead played a significant role in navigation of this kind. But from the south coast of the North Sea, which was in many ways similar to the south Baltic coast, the use of leads in the Viking and early medieval periods can be demonstrated by the discovery of a lead at Dorestad and by the depiction of the use of such a device in two scenes in the Bayeux Tapestry. When west European ships began to sail into the Baltic round Skagen in the thirteenth century, the lead was an important help in allowing cogs to navigate the Danish narrows safely. This is shown by the *Seebuch*, a description of sailing routes compiled in Hamburg in the fifteenth century from older material. What is more, the lead remained an important help in fixing the location of sailing ships even after the compass was commonly used.

Both Ohthere and Wulfstan navigated Danish waters without the aid of a compass over a thousand years ago. The information they gave Alfred about the routes, and the times taken, stands up to critical examination which takes account of what is now known about the coasts and the technology that was then available to seamen. These careful, firsthand accounts are very different from the geographical and ethnological surveys, often obscure, distorted or mythical, with which the translator of Orosius supplemented his text in order to furnish a description of these lands that were so remote from south and western Europe.

Translated by P. H. Sawyer.

Ohthere and Viking Age Trade

P. H. SAWYER

Long before the time of Ohthere and Wulfstan, Scandinavia and the Baltic were important as a region from which the rulers and aristocrats of Europe could obtain exotic things that served as symbols of their power and prestige. In Dark Age Europe one of the hall-marks of nobility was the ostentatious display of wealth, coupled with open-handed generosity to friends and followers who deserved it. Rich people then, as now, delighted in having beautiful and unusual possessions whose value was enhanced by rarity, and such things were appropriate as gifts. Exotic goods of this kind could be obtained from many parts of the world but for western Europe one important and relatively accessible source was the Baltic and the lands beyond it, Scandinavia, northern Russia and the Arctic. The tribute extorted by Ohthere from the Lapps gives a good indication of some of the more valuable exports of the far north: furs – marten, otter and bear, skins of reindeer and seal, and feathers. Walrus ivory appears to have been something that Ohthere and his companions hunted for themselves.

Animal skins and furs have always been an important element in clothing and although fur-bearing animals are found in all parts of Europe, the best furs come from the coldest regions. In the fourteenth-century markets of London and Bruges the highest prices were paid for the grey-backed skins of the winter squirrel imported from Novgorod, and three centuries earlier Adam of Bremen was well aware both of the abundance of furs in the Baltic lands and of the high value put on them by his German contemporaries. He records that in Norway 'there are black foxes and hares, white martens and bears of the same colour who live under the water'. He describes the Pruzzi, living south of the Baltic, as having 'an abundance of strange furs, the odour of which has inoculated our world with the deadly poison of pride. These furs they regard as dung, to our shame, I believe, for right or wrong we hanker after a martenskin robe as much as for supreme happiness', while the Swedes 'regard as nothing every means of vainglory; that is gold, silver, stately chargers, beaver and marten pelts, which make us lose our minds admiring them'. The importance of Scandinavia as a source of furs was recognised in the sixth century. The Byzantine historian Jordanes reported that the Svear, or Swedes, were 'famed for the dark beauty of their furs' and

The Franks Casket. A whalebone casket with reliefs carved in Northumbria about 700 AD. The scenes are mythological, biblical, and historical. One side shows a scene from the Weland legend. Also shown are the Adoration of the Magi, Romulus and Remus sucking the wolf, and Titus' conquest of Jerusalem in 70 AD. These scenes are explained in inscriptions partly in runes, partly in Roman characters. The lid and three sides are now in the British Museum, presented to it in 1867 by Sir A.W. Franks. The missing side is in the Museo Nazionale *at Florence. Height 10.5 cm. length 23 cm. width 18.5 cm.*
Photo: The British Museum.

that they exported their 'sapphire coloured skins' to the Roman world.

Another material that was in great demand was ivory, for rings and other ornaments or as a beautiful and costly substitute for wood in making such objects as book covers or caskets. When elephant tusks became very scarce, after the fifth century, whalebone or walrus tusks were used instead, and until the discovery of Greenland the only source of the latter was the Arctic north of Norway. These materials were used for some important objects; the Franks casket in the British Museum is made of whalebone and the eighth-century Gandersheim casket was made somewhere in England. Another highly prized material was amber, and although deposits of this fossil resin are found in many parts of Europe, the most abundant sources are round the south of the Baltic, and in Jutland. Baltic amber was being exported to the Mediterranean in the Bronze Age and in the first century AD Pliny describes how a Roman knight, commissioned to obtain amber for a gladiatorial display, travelled to the Baltic and collected 'so plentiful a supply that the nets used for keeping the beasts away from the parapet of the amphitheatre were knotted with pieces of amber, and the arms, biers (for dead gladiators) and all the equipment used on one day, the display each day being varied, had amber fittings'. The largest piece was said to weigh 13 pounds. Pliny also reports that amber 'was imported every day of our lives and floods the market'. Some was re-exported to the Persian Empire and this 'Roman' amber was highly valued in China. The Persians also imported furs from Russia, and their demand led to the precocious development of some areas long before the ninth century. The valley of the river Kama, for example, was relatively rich in the sixth and seventh centuries, with a settled population, large grave fields and hill forts. Sassanian and Byzantine silver has been found there, presumably imported in exchange for furs and other Arctic produce. There are indications that the Arctic valley of the Pechora river was at that time being exploited by men from the Kama region in much the same way as it was in a later period.

By controlling the export of northern produce, the rulers or chieftains of Scandinavia were able to acquire, in return, precious goods from the south. When Rome dominated western Europe, significant quantities of Roman luxury goods reached Scandinavia and have been recovered from richly furnished graves; glass bowls and beakers, cauldrons and other large bronze vessels, jugs, bowls and ladles of silver or bronze, jewellery, fine pottery and weapons. Some may have been brought back by people who had spent some time in the empire, as servants, soldiers or even honoured guests, and some of the best pieces may well have been diplomatic gifts, but there is no reason to doubt that some reached Scandinavia by way of trade, in exchange for amber, furs, slaves and other exports of the north.

The collapse of Roman imperial authority in the west, and the subsequent struggle for power in Europe, certainly had great effects, both direct and indirect in Scandinavia as the demand for northern products declined. Imports from the Roman world and from the former Roman provinces still reached Scandinavia but the quantities were much smaller in the fifth and sixth centuries than earlier. The land routes across Europe were disrupted at that time but the sea route from the west was open and in the fifth century an increasing number of western imports reached Jutland and Norway.

Western Europe was also disrupted by the collapse of Roman power but Gaul recovered quickly under its new Frankish rulers who brought under their protection the old Roman markets and encouraged the development of new ones. The largest and most important of these was Dorestad, well placed to control traffic along the Rhine and with good access, thanks to a network of waterways, to both the Meuse and the north Frisian coast. The market established there by the Franks in the seventh century grew to become the largest and most active trading centre of the eighth century in northern Europe. It had a river frontage of some two kilometres, tightly packed with wharves or landing stages. It was also a major craft centre; ships were built or repaired there, weapons and jewellery were made, and so too was cloth, and there is abundant evidence of bone and amber working. Large quantities of imports from the Rhineland have been found there, including high quality pottery, mill-stones and barrels that probably once contained wine. From Dorestad goods like these were exported to other parts of the Frankish world, to England and to Scandinavia. Similar markets flourished at the same time elsewhere in Frankia and in England, although none rivalled Dorestad in size. It was through these places that goods were taken to and from Scandinavia, a trade that certainly grew dramatically in the eighth century. The goods imported from Scandinavia were much the same as they had been in Roman times but seem to have included, in addition to luxuries, such useful Norwegian exports as whetstones and soap-stone, which could be shaped into cooking pots and other vessels. It is also possible that iron was exported. Iron production was increasing in many parts of Scandinavia at that time and some may have been shipped overseas, although so far no direct evidence for such exports has been found.

The pagan burials of Scandinavia suggest that there was a significant increase in imports from western Europe in the eighth century. This is best seen in the relative abundance of western glass in the form of bowls and beakers, that was buried in the eighth-century Swedish boat graves. The excavations at Ribe, in south-west Jutland, show that craftsmen were active there in the first half of the eighth century working with bronze, iron, antler, bone, leather, glass and amber. Ribe's contacts with the west are evidenced not only by the glass, pottery and mill-stones, but also by the discovery there of 32 silver coins, some of which certainly came from Dorestad. These form part of a rapidly growing body of coin evidence for eighth-century contact between western Europe, especially Frisia, and western Denmark. Eighth-century imports from western Europe have also been found at Helgö in Lake Mälaren which, like Ribe, was a place in which craftsmen worked.

The growing demand in western Europe for northern goods had two direct consequences, both reflected in the accounts of the voyages of Ohthere and Wulfstan. First, it led some men to

The Gandersheim Casket. Walrus ivory or whalebone with lock and mounts of bronze. The style of the carvings is known in many parts of England in the late eighth or early ninth centuries. The casket is now in the Herzog Anton Ulrich-Museum in Brunswick and it is supposed to have come there from the nearby monastery of Gandersheim. Since this is pure conjecture some scholars prefer to call it the Brunswick casket. Height and Length 12.6 cm. width 6.8 cm.

Photo: Herzog Anton Ulrich-Museum, Braunschweig. (Museumsfoto B.P. Keiser).

Comb of walrus ivory. The area between the two rows of teeth is decorated, on one side with a pair of confronting biped animals of Anglo-Saxon ancestry, on the other with an interlacing snake-like animal in the Scandinavian Ringerike style. An interesting example of the contact between Anglo-Saxon and Viking art, probably from the first half of the eleventh century. Provenance unknown. Length 5.4 cm. width 4.1 cm. Photo: The British Museum.

go far afield in search of new supplies. Ohthere himself explained that his journey round North Cape was undertaken partly out of curiosity but 'mainly for the walruses for they have very fine ivory in their tusks', while the part of the Baltic coast visited by Wulfstan had long been exploited by raiders, or traders, Swedes and others, who came by sea. Secondly, it led to the development of trading centres or markets in Scandinavia and around the Baltic. Three are mentioned in the texts translated here; *Sciringesheal*, identified as Kaupang in Vestfold, Hedeby and Truso. Others are mentioned in the ninth-century *Life of St Anskar*, the bishop of Hamburg who worked as a missionary in both Denmark and Sweden. He visited the great market of Birka in Lake Mäleren and there met merchants who were familiar with the journey to Dorestad and he was also responsible for founding churches at both

Two angels carved in walrus ivory. They are said to have been found in a garden in Winchester and probably come from a small casket or portable altar on which they formed part of a representation of Christ in Majesty. Late tenth century. Height 7.5 cm. greatest width 5 cm.
Photo: Winchester City Museum.

Hedeby and Ribe. Rimbert explains that when the church was built at Hedeby there was great joy there because merchants from both Saxony and Dorestad then 'made for the place readily and without any fear – something which was not possible previously – and at that time there was an abundant supply of goods of every kind'.

Hedeby, visited by both Ohthere and Wulfstan, had close contacts, by sea, with the lands around the Baltic and with Norway. It was also connected by road, the 'Army' – or 'Ox-street' with Saxony. As Rimbert's *Life of Anskar* shows, it was also visited by merchants from Dorestad and was therefore in touch with western Europe. The route between Hedeby and Dorestad was never described in detail. Some travellers may have crossed Jutland by land and continued their journey from Hollingsted or nearby, but merchants with bulky or heavy cargoes are more likely to have sailed through Limfjord along which there are many indications of eighth-century activity, most notably at Lindholm Høje. There is nothing in Ohthere's account of his journeys to suggest that he travelled through Hedeby on his way to England; a more natural route from western Norway would have been directly across the North Sea, like the pirates who first attacked the British Isles in the eighth century.

There were other markets in the Baltic, one of the earliest and most important being Staraja Ladoga, controlling, or guarding, one of the main routes from the Baltic into the rich fur- and

slave-gathering region of north Russia. The earlier contacts between that region and the Byzantine and Persian empires had been disrupted in the mid-seventh century by the expansion of Islam. After their conquest of Iran the Caliphs attempted, with great violence but without success, to control the area north of the Caucasus and as a result the traffic that passed through that region was interrupted. By the end of the eighth century, however, the situation had improved sufficiently for Iranian and other Islamic merchants to make their way to the markets on the river Volga, and there is good evidence in the ninth century and later for northern imports into the Caliphate including slaves and furs. The Muslims also obtained from the Arctic what they called 'fish teeth', that is, walrus tusks. Some of these furs, and all the ivory was obtained from Finns and others who lived in the far north. There is a tenth-century Persian account of contacts between the trading centres that then flourished on the middle Volga and 'the savage people of the north' to whom the traders took salt, clothes and other things in sledges drawn by dogs. One of these northern peoples was said to trade 'by means of signs and dumb show, for they are wild and afraid of men. From them are imported excellent sables and other fine furs; they hunt these animals, feeding on their flesh and wearing their skins'.

Ohthere himself encountered Finns in the Kola peninsula. In Old English they were called *Beormas*, representing an Old Norse *Bjarmar*, which derived from a Finnish word *perm* that was used for travelling merchants. The same Finnish word was also used for another group of traders who operated further east, between the Volga and the Arctic, and has consequently been applied to their territory and survives as the name of a Russian province, Perm. There were other

Aerial view of Ohthere's Sciringesheal, *later known as Kaupang, at the Viksfjord southeast of Larvik. Since the first excavation was undertaken in 1867 archaeological work has been going on at intervals, and an extensive investigation was made by Charlotte Blindheim in the years 1950-70. This covered both grave-fields, some of which had been studied earlier, and the settlement areas, which had not. These excavations have established the existence here from c.800 till sometime in the tenth century of a port with houses and quays, and finds, particularly pottery and coins, show that the place had connections with both Western and Eastern Europe. Our knowledge of* Sciringesheal *and its history is, however, far from complete. Only three percent of its total of 40.000 m² has been studied and it is therefore difficult to judge whether it was a seasonal market or whether it was permanently occupied. The coastline has changed considerably since the ninth century, the ground having risen several metres.*
Photo: Universitetets Oldsaksamling, Oslo.

52

Aerial view of Hedeby. Ohthere's æt Hæðum has been identified as the predecessor of Schleswig, situated on the south side of the Schlei at the cove of Haddeby. In Frankish sources it was called Sliaswic *or* Sliestorp, *in Danish sources* Hedeby, Haiþabu. *It was one of the first towns in the proper sense of the word to emerge in Scandinavia. Goods from Western and Eastern Europe and from Norway and Sweden have been found there and many different craftsmen worked in the town: combmakers, amber polishers, gold- and silver-smiths etc. Excavations have been going on for decades and although only five percent of the total area has been uncovered they have yielded a good picture of the town laid out along the brook and of its houses and wooden pavements. An urban settlement from before 800 AD has been found south of the semicircular rampart but in 808 AD King Godfred forcibly removed the merchants from the Abodrite port of* Reric, *perhaps near later* Lübeck, *to Hedeby and they were probably settled in the centre. Excavations have traced individual plots back to c.800 and, as in York, they remained unchanged for centuries. The rampart was not there when Ohthere visited the place; it was built in the first half of the tenth century.*

The most recent excavations were carried out in the harbour. Viking-Age merchants did not just pull their ships ashore, Sciringesheal *had a quay and so did Hedeby. Two piers have been found and at the end of one of them the wreck of a large merchant ship was found. The harbour yielded many other exciting finds, too, for what was lost into its muddy water was not easily recovered. In the town itself very few coins were found but the harbour yielded sixty-nine.*

Hedeby covered an area of 240.000 m² inside the rampart, six times the area of Sciringesheal. *Even though its settlement area may not at any time have been fully occupied it was certainly a very large town by contemporary standards. York, of course, was bigger but Hedeby matched the size of* Hamwih *the predecessor of Southampton.*

groups exploiting the Arctic, including the *Cwenas* (Old Norse *Kvenir*), also Finnish. Ohthere mentions them and emphasised their conflicts with the Norwegians. These Finnish traders may themselves have hunted but they probably relied for most of their supplies on tribute taken from the native Lapps, as Ohthere himself did. Icelandic sagas preserve some echoes of contacts between Norwegians and Bjarmar, Kvenir and other traders, and with the Lapps. In *St Olaf's saga*, for example, there is a story about a trading expedition to the Dvina that ended with the sanctuary of the Bjarmar being plundered and their god, Jomali, destroyed. There is also a story in *Egil's saga* about an alliance between Norwegians and Kvenir against Karelians.

The account of Ohthere's activities provides a precious glimpse of ninth-century Norway and it confirms what archaeological evidence suggests, that there was a lively demand for northern produce. It was this that led Norwegians to colonise the far north, just as Swedes from Mälardalen were at the same time colonising the northern coasts of the Gulf of Bothnia. Ohthere's report to Alfred also reveals something of the complicated situation in this remote region as rival groups, Swedes, Norwegians and Finns, competed, and sometimes cooperated, to exploit the riches of the Arctic, in part by extorting tribute from the native Lapps, a process that has continued until modern times.

Picture of a Norwegian peasant with a walrus rope, taken in the 1950s. Walrus rope has remained in use in northern Norway till our own day and at the beginning of the century it was found on every farm. It was considered stronger than all other rope and was used for special tasks, such as to girth timber or a hayload, to suspend church bells, and in recent times for driving-belts in threshers. Olaus Magnus tells that walrus rope was also used to assemble huge siege machines and he describes how it was provided: when a walrus had stranded, its skin was loosened at the tail and tied to the ground. The men then threw stones at the walrus so that it would try to reach the water, thereby skinning itself. From northern Norway it is reported that walruses were skinned spiralwise, beginning at the tail. In this way it was possible to get 60 ells of rope from an animal only 7 ells long.

In the later Middle Ages it was believed that the walrus rosmarus *was caught while it lay sleeping on the rocks (Pedersen 1951).*

Some questions of language

CHRISTINE E. FELL

We do not know what language Ohthere was speaking when he gave King Alfred his account of his voyages. He himself may have acquired reasonably fluent Old English – a merchant would have to have some quickness at languages, and he has some idea about the possible relationship of the tongues spoken by *Finnas* and *Beormas*. The *Beormas* told him many stories but we do not know which language was the medium for communication. On the other hand King Alfred and some of the men at his court, in the course of long and wearying treaties with the Danes, may have acquired a certain familiarity with Old Norse. There is clear evidence of words finding their way from one language to another, which is not suggestive of matters being handled by formal translators. The Anglo-Saxons heard enough from the Vikings about *grið* to incorporate the word into their own language. The Icelandic poet who introduced the Old English word *portgerefa* into a poem about Óláfr helgi in the Norse form *portgreifi* demonstrates that the Vikings too heard certain strategic words sufficiently often to adopt them into their own language. The two languages were at this date still moderately close, close enough for a number of simple words and constructions to sound fairly similar. Some philological competence is demonstrated by the fact that writers of Old Norse tend to treat Old English personal names as if the elements were Norse not English. We know that when Old English *ā* occurs in a word like *stān* we shall find in Old Norse a form with *ei* – *steinn*. That Norsemen too could make this simple deduction is demonstrated by their spelling in the sagas of the personal name Æthelstan as Aðalsteinn.

Other words which were cognates may have developed different meanings in the two languages, and here too we have evidence that people using these languages were aware of such differences. The shift of meaning in Old English *eorl* to a sense approximating more closely to Old Norse *jarl* is an obvious example. Clearly Ohthere may have been using an interpreter, but the evidence of the text is I think against it. In the first place the description of Alfred as Ohthere's *hlaford*, his 'lord' implies something more formal and of longer duration than Dr Niels Lund allows. In the second place the text carries in itself the implications both of the questions behind the answers, and of the occasional fumbling for words which hesitant communication would necessitate. It is noticeable that there is no such feeling present in the subsequent account of Wulfstan's voyage, which, though it is so personal that the record slides into direct speech, and though it makes occasional curiously abrupt transitions, is very much more fluent and less repetitive than Ohthere's.

It is necessary in reading the account of Ohthere's voyages to assess how much we can learn from the actual language of the text in front of us. Two factors that emerge are the hidden – or not so hidden – presence of the interrogator, and the discovery that Old English evidently did not have words for all the information that Ohthere was trying to convey.

Dr Lund has presented one rationale for the reiterated phrase 'the land turned or the sea penetrated the land, he did not know which'. A moment's reflection on Norwegian geography suggests an alternative explanation. Ohthere probably said that it was not clear to him whether the land-mass had turned and he was following the coast-line, or whether he had entered an enormous fjord which he would subsequently have to sail out of again. Doubtless the Anglo-Saxons had some word for an inlet but nothing close to the Old Norse *fjörðr* – a word without which Norwegians would be at a considerable loss in describing their own environment. If the interrogator were obliged to ask Ohthere for a definition of this word, it would obviously emerge as a place where the sea penetrates the land – which is what the text says. It is significant that present-day English has had to adopt the modern Norwegian word because of precisely the same language deficiency.

A similar examination by a patient interviewer of the precise implications of Ohthere's account is demonstrated in the opening paragraphs. The emphasis on who lives where, and on what are settlement-sites and what are camp-sites represents a distinction drawn by Ohthere between two ways of living, preserved in the written report by the verbs *buan* and *wician* both translatable as 'to live'. The distinction between the verbs is that *buan* tends to be used of permanent accommodation, *wician* of temporary camps. In a casual reading of the text Ohthere appears to be saying that no-one lived to the north of him but the *Finnas* lived to the north of him. It may have sounded a little like that to his original audience as well. There is therefore this careful and repetitive probing of the distinction between the settled areas of the Norwegians and the *Beormas*, and the vast areas in between where there are no permanent settlement sites, but there are the temporary camps of nomadic *Finnas*.

We detect the interrogator at work again in the curious syntax of the statement 'he said that a man could not sail (to Sciringesheal) in a month'. It is odd for a man to say how long it did not take him to complete a voyage. It makes perfect sense however as the answer to an unrecorded question 'Could you do it in a month?', formulated roughly as 'Well, no I don't think so, not even with a favourable wind'.

Ohthere's description of the fauna of his country also leads him and his interrogator into difficulties. I am not absolutely sure that the audience recognised his name as the cognate form of their own word *otr*, but there is a spelling of this as *octur* in the Épinal-Erfurt glossary. It seems clear however that his audience are not familiar with the walrus or the reindeer – as indeed why should they be – and he has to describe the creature and provide the terminology. This is the only recorded instance in Old English of the term *horshwæl* 'walrus' (literally 'horse-whale') and its unfamiliarity may be demonstrated by the difficulty that the scribe of the Tollemache manuscript has with the spelling. We note that he also had trouble with the unfamiliar tribal name *Beormas* causing him to write *beornas*.

There can be no possible reason for the Anglo-Saxons to have heard of walruses. Ohthere's description of it as 'this whale is much smaller than other whales' is directed to an ignorant audience, and the word *horshwæl* must be a newly coined compound based on Ohthere's name for the creature. What Anglo-Saxons are familiar with are the general words for whale *hwæl* and *hron*. They normally use *hwæl* for Latin *cetus* and *hron* for *ballena* but not consistently. In one glossary *ballena vel cetus vel piscatrix* is *hwæl*, in another *ballena* is *hron oð ðe hwæl*. The Franks casket announces itself to be *hronæs ban*, i.e. whalebone. The walrus on the other hand would obviously be known to the inhabitants of north-ern Scandinavia and it is natural that Old Norse should have a far greater range of words for whales (including the walrus) than are found in Anglo-Saxon England. Snorri's *Edda* offers us a total of twenty-six against the Old English total of two, and even allowing for the fact that some may be poetic synonyms others are clearly names for different kinds of whale. Eighteen of these occur in the Norse text *Konungs Skuggsjá* which has several others not in the *Edda*. Both lists include the *hrosshvalr* though there is much scholarly discussion on whether this was in fact a name for the walrus, or for a kind of whale. Two other Norse words *rostungr* and *rosmhvalr* are names for the walrus. The other northern creature from which ivory may be obtained is the narwhale (Old Norse *náhvalr*) and this word too we have eventually borrowed from Norse sources. The beast which Ohthere pursued because it had very excellent bone in its teeth must have been walrus or narwhale and the Old English *horshwæl* suggests the etymon *hrosshvalr*. It cannot obviously have been *náhvalr*, but it is not impossible that it should have been *rosmhvalr* with the Anglo-Saxons mishearing the first syllable and producing a false etymology. Or Ohthere may not have discriminated clearly himself, or there may have been a later semantic shift in the Old Norse usage. Our Old English text of Ohthere antedates recorded Old Norse forms of these words by several centuries. What the Anglo-Saxons thought Ohthere said was evidently *hrosshvalr*. They had in Old English

One of the earliest drawings of a walrus, taken from a report which has travelled all the way from the White Sea to Western Europe (Pedersen 1951).

both elements of the compound and only a very slight linguistic skill is required for Ohthere or his interrogator to produce a compound word in Old English analogous to the existing one in Norse. That the Anglo-Saxons themselves should have independently developed the term *horshwæl* for a beast that lives in Arctic waters, and that their Biblical and classical literary sources would not supply a word for is not credible. Even Isidore of Seville writes of ivory only as elephant ivory.

When Anglo-Saxons write about ivory the texts refer to elephant ivory not walrus ivory, whatever the actual commodity in circulation. Two phrases found regularly are *elpen-* or *ylpenban* 'elephant-bone' and *hrones ban* or *hwæles ban* 'whalebone'. Walrus ivory is distinguishable both from whalebone and from elephant ivory, and in modern technical usage the terms whalebone and whale-bone are further distinguished as referring to different parts of the skeletal anatomy. But we have to be cautious about the absurdity of imposing such precise distinctions on Anglo-Saxon terminology. Before Alfred's reign we can find a number of objects in Anglo-Saxon England carved from bone and from ivory, but so far as archaeologists can tell us the early pieces do not include known objects identified as walrus-ivory. The Gandersheim box of dubious provenance is commonly so described, but Leslie Webster of the Department of Medieval and Later Antiquities in the British Museum points out in a private communication that it is time for this uncritical assessment to be subjected to scientific tests, and that the box may well be *hronæs ban*. Mrs. Webster comments further that she has not been able to identify one piece of walrus ivory decorative carving before the tenth century among Anglo-Saxon 'ivories'. In the tenth and eleventh centuries however there is much more carved walrus-ivory in Anglo-Saxon England and it is reasonable to view these pieces as examples of a new pattern in North Sea trading opened up by Viking contacts and settlement. It is perfectly possible that *þa teð hie brohton sume þæm cyninge* were the earliest pieces of walrus ivory that found their way to Anglo-Saxon England, and therefore no reason to assume that the Anglo-Saxons viewed them as anything other than high quality *hwæles ban*. There is no independent term developed in Old English for walrus-ivory, which means that when the term *hwales ban* is used later in the Ohthere text we have no means of knowing how we should translate it. In the list of tribute paid by *Finnas*

This curious beast is Rosmarus norvegicus. *Its powerful cylindrical tail suggests some prehistoric creature; but the walrus is indicated, not only by the name, but also by the tusks, correctly placed in the upper jaw (Pedersen 1951).*

three out of the four commodities are in the plural; skins of beasts, feathers of birds and shipropes: *hwales ban* is in the singular. I am not aware of any analogous term for ivory in Old Norse, and in the absence of precise distinctions in Old English terminology between walrus-ivory and whalebone we cannot know which of the two is meant at this point. The difference which would doubtless have been perfectly clear to a Norwegian like Ohthere, may not have been equally clear to an Anglo-Saxon interrogator and it is not proper to impose a distinction here which he may not have had sufficient knowledge to make. A likely interpretation of the text is that the tribute was walrus ivory, and that Ohthere's initial voyage was an attempt to locate the source of supply.

Whether or not Ohthere's walrus tusks were the first seen at Alfred's court – and this makes good sense in view of the care taken to record the event – it is probable that from this period onwards both walrus ivory and narwhale ivory were freely imported both in their natural state and in finished objects. Artefacts survive, but what Ohthere brought were 'teeth' not objects made from them.

The phrase *swiþe æþele ban on hiora toþum* 'excellent bone in their teeth' is also worth investigating. The Old English word *æðele* is most commonly used of people in the sense 'noble', and is more rarely used of inanimate things. Old Norse *aðal-* is used as the first element of many compounds where its implication is 'foremost' or 'most important' and it is possible that the implication of Ohthere's statement is that he had located the best quality material, as the German cognate *edel* is used for 'precious' metal and 'precious' stones. The full phrase also suggests a conflation between the nomenclature for ivory of Norsemen and Anglo-Saxons. The common word for ivory in Old Norse is 'tooth', *tann* or *tönn* on its own or in compounds. *Tannbagall* is 'a crozier of walrus ivory', *tannhjölt* 'a hilt of walrus ivory'. There are words too for the carver's craft and tools. *Tannari* is 'a tusk-chisel', *grafa tönn* is 'to carve ivory', the merchant's goods include *tannvara*. In Old and early Middle English however the word 'tooth' would be aberrant and all phrases for ivory use the word 'bone', just as modern Scandinavian and German retain the term 'elephant-bone' *elfenben/elfenbein* for ivory of whatever source without regard to the actual nature of the material. Middle English has a variety of phrases, none of them very helpful, since in poetic similes it can make little difference what commodity the poet has in mind whether he compares a girl's skin to *whales bone* or *alpes bon*. But unless *rewell bone* can be pressed into service as a corrupt form of 'narwhale bone' there is no source I know of that refers precisely to ivory obtained from any northern sea-beast other than the indiscriminate 'whale', and no source either that suggests ivory is obtained from tusks as distinct from bone. This is in direct contrast to the references for example to boars' tusks. There are entries in both Old and Middle English medicinal recipes which require the use of both boars' tusks and ivory; 'mid hilpen bane and mid bares twuxe'; or 'mid heortes horne and mid ylpen bane and mid bares tuxe', which shows clearly the proper distinction between the use of the words 'horn' and 'tusk' but retains the generalised 'bone' in the phrase for ivory. The absence of an Old Norse cognate to Old English *tux* 'tusk' may also be the reason why our text has the less exact word 'teeth'. But it is clearly another comment on the greater precision of Ohthere's knowledge and terminology than that of his audience that he would naturally describe his gift to the king as 'teeth' and they would automatically think of it as bone – *swiþe æþele ban on hiora toþum.*

Hran for 'reindeer' is another word that is unrecorded elsewhere in Old English. Middle and Modern English have adopted the word in its Norwegian form (*rayne-dere* occurs circa 1400) and the Old English word here is clearly a translation of Old Norse *hreinn.* The speakers have recognised that if Old Norse has *ei* Old English should have an analogous form with a long *a*. If the cognate does not exist it can be invented. Whether *stælhran* is another such loan is a subject of some debate since it is difficult to decide the etymon of the first element.

There may very easily be other concealed loan-words of this type in the prose of Ohthere's voyages. The word 'ell' existed in both Old English and Old Norse and is obviously one for which any traders would be very careful to ensure they understood variation of meaning. It has recently been argued that the word in this text must represent an Old English ell of nearly two feet rather than the Old Norse norm of eighteen inches but this is obviously something that would have had to be thought through by speaker and interrogator. The word *kyrtel* on the other hand, which also was common to both Old Norse and Old English, may have slid into the account without anyone asking whether the word invariably referred to the same garment in the two languages. I have translated it 'jacket' which seems appropriate to the frequent Old Norse use of *kyrtill* for the short top garment worn by men.

In *Njáls saga* where Gunnarr sees an enemy go past, he simply catches a glimpse of a red *kyrtill*, which must, in this instance, be a short tunic. On the other hand in *Gísla saga* the women wear *kyrtlar* which trail on the ground, *draga kyrtlarnir döggslóðina.* In Old English however, the word is regularly used of a full-length woman's dress as the wills of women demonstrate. A dress of bearskin would be uncomfortable, heavy and hot, but it is possible that Ohthere and his interviewer did not trouble themselves here with precise definition. *Kyrtel* does not stand out as an obvious loan word in the way that *dreng* and *grið* do in *The Battle of Maldon,* but its semantic range here may reflect Old Norse rather than Old English usage.

Skill in finding appropriate Old English forms for borrowed words may be seen also in the handling of place-names. English *æt Hæðum* may have already existed or may be a translation of *haiþa bu* the place on the heaths. It is noticeable that both Old English and Old Norse have the plural. A later Anglo-Saxon writer Æthelweard simply takes over the Scandinavian word: 'quod sermone Saxonico Slesuuic nuncupatur secundum vero Danos, Haithaby'. The Norse form was not however acceptable to the man recording Ohthere's voyage. *Sciringesheal* has usually been taken to be an Anglicised form of Old Norse *Skiringssalr* with the assumption that the second element meant 'hall'. However the grammar of the Old English form implies a masculine second element *healh,* and it is besides hard to see why an original *salr* should not have been Anglicised as *sele* using the cognate word, since *sele* is perfectly possible as an Old English place-name element. *Heall* 'hall' is exceedingly rare in pre-Conquest English place-names whereas *healh* is common in the general sense of 'a nook or corner of land' or with a more precise topographical meaning, and to an Anglo-Saxon writing in the ninth century it would make perfect sense as a place-name element. We cannot however recover the exact Old Norse form on which it is based, and by the time we hear of a trading station in this location from our Scandinavian sources, the word is *Kaupang* 'market'. The whole pattern is in significant contrast to the subsequent account of Wulfstan's voyage where the form *Sconeg*, for example, obviously is intended to represent Old Norse *Skáney*, though the Old English *Scedenig* existed and is known to us from *Beowulf*.

Ohthere's statement that he did not enter Beormian waters *for unfriþe* is one I examine at some length in my forthcoming article in *Saga-Book of the Viking Society* vol. XXI, part 1. All previous translators have offered some variant on the phrase 'for fear of hostility'. My examination of the evidence leads me to the conclusion that to have *frið* meant to have formal trading rights and agreements, and the absence of *frið* is more properly construed as the absence of an entry permit, than as enmity. I ought also to explain here my translation of *plega* in the Wulfstan passage as 'gambling', since there is no over-whelming evidence to justify it. My reasons are mainly common-sense ones. I have never found the vague translations 'sports' or 'festivities' convincing in this context, and it seems much more plausible that people gambled away the dead man's property. Tacitus has something to say about the prevalence of gambling among Germanic tribes, but comments also that they have only one kind of public show (*Germania* 24) and that those who practise it are not paid for it. This supports my conviction that it would be difficult to work out what 'festivities' could use up so much money among the *Este*. *Plega* literally 'play' in the text is in the singular not plural, and 'play' in the sense of gambling is recorded in early Middle English. It must therefore have been present in Old English, and the difficulty about recognising it in this sense is simply the wide semantic range of the word. When the Laws object to drinking and *plega* in churches we may suspect that *plega* means dicing rather than other pastimes, but there is no proof. I suggest 'gambling' for *plega* in the Wulfstan passage as making rather better sense than the usual translation but I cannot adduce powerful documentary support.

Finally I record my disagreement with Dr Lund on the matter of *Iraland*. It seems to me highly likely that Ohthere spoke of *Ísland*, and not at all improbable that a West-Saxon scribe should have got it wrong. It may indicate one of the times when communication between Ohthere and his interrogator remained unsuccessful.

Notes

AFDREDE: The Abodrites, a Slav tribe occupying West Mecklenburg and East Holstein. About 800 AD they were the allies of Charlemagne against the Saxons and the Danes. In 808 the Danish king Godfred (?810) forced the majority of them into submission and made them tributary to him. On the same occasion he forcibly transferred the merchants from their unidentified port of *Reric* to his own *Sliastorp*, the continental name of Hedeby.

BEORMAS: The name of the inhabitants in an area round the White Sea, known as Bjarmaland. The word is a loan from Finnish, in Finnish dialects a *permi* being a travelling merchant from Outer Karelia. These merchants bought goods, mostly furs, in the whole of northern Russia and sold them to the Volga-Bulgars who again had trade links with the Muslim world, and Arab coins of the tenth century have been found along the trade routes of the Beormas.

BEHEMAS, BEME: Bohemia was conquered by Charlemagne, and in the ninth century it was nominally under Frankish suzerainty, except for a period during which the duke of Bohemia acknowledged Prince Svatopluk of Moravia as his overlord. Then as now the capital of Bohemia was Prague.

BÆGWÆRE: The Bavarians. For a long period Bavaria was an independent duchy under Frankish overlordship. In 763 Duke Tassilo rid himself of that overlordship but was subjugated again by Charlemagne in 788, and Bavaria was then incorporated in the Carolingian Empire. When that was divided in 843 Bavaria became the most important province in East Frankia, and Louis the German (843-876) and Arnulf (887-899) resided in Regensburg.

CARENDRE: Carinthia, a province of present day Austria. In the mid-eighth century Duke Tassilo of Bavaria conquered Carinthia from the Avars, and till 976 it formed part of Bavaria. The population consisted of Slovenians, a South Slavonic tribe.

CWENAS:
CWENLAND:
CWENSÆ: The *Cwenas*, in Old West Norse *Kvenir*, were a Finnish tribe or confraternity who from the ninth to the twelfth centuries undertook hunting, trading, tribute-taking, and plundering raids as far as Lappland and the Finnmark. They were the predecessors of the *Birkarlar* who later controlled the trade in northern Scandinavia and took tribute from the Lapps. In his *History of the Archbishops of Hamburg* Adam of Bremen has an account of their recurrent attacks on the Swedes that reads much like Ohthere's information about their raids on the Norwegians. They are also mentioned in *Egill Skallagrímsson's saga*.

Since these *Cwenas* operated over most of the Arctic area *Cwensæ* is probably the White Sea but the Gulf of Bothnia has been suggested by scholars locating them in the region north and north-east of that. The name does not seem to have been in current use in the ninth century and may have been invented for this occasion.

DALAMENTSAN: A Slavic tribe living on both shores of the Elbe northwest of Dresden, roughly between Meissen and Mühlberg. It must be an error, therefore, when the text locates them *northeast* of the Moravians; it should be northwest. According to the *Annals of Fulda* Louis the German subjugated them in 856 with the help of the Sorbs. When in 880 they learnt that the Germans had suffered a severe defeat at the hands of the Vikings they unsuccessfully tried to rid themselves of German overlordship.

DANES: The introduction distinguishes between South-Danes and North-Danes. This distinction is not found in other sources and no known political or ethnographical realities explain it. We have no indications that in the ninth century Denmark was divided in two, or that two tribes of Danes could be distinguished, but on the other hand there is no evidence that rules out these possibilities. It is worth noting, though, that this distinction is not made in Ohthere's accounts and he after all had travelled in the country.

DATIA: The Roman province of Dacia north of the Danube, now split between Hungary and Romania. Under the emperor Aurelian (270-75) the Romans abandoned Dacia which was taken over by the Visigoths, a Germanic tribe subsequently forced by the Huns to continue its migration and finally to settle in Spain in the fifth century. Throughout the Middle Ages Hungary was often called Dacia although after the Visigoths had left the population was first Huns, later Avars and after the end of the ninth century Magyars.

ESTE: See *Witland.*

ESTMERE: An 80 km long lagoon in the south-eastern part of the bay of Gdansk. It is known in German as *Frisches Haff.* It is separated from the Baltic by a long narrow peninsula consisting of dunes and has an outlet to the sea at Pillau in the north. This outlet was formed by a storm in 1510; in the Viking period it had an opening at the western end. In Polish *Estmere* is called *Zalew Wislany,* the delta of the Vistula, and that river sends numerous branches into it. Today the Vistula has a main fall directly into the bay of Gdansk at Gdansk but formerly all branches fell into the *Zalew Wislany.*

FINNAS: See *Scridefinnas.*

HÅLGOLAND: Hålgoland, the northernmost province of Norway, mostly lying north of the Polar circle. Precisely where Ohthere lived is unknown but he may quite possibly have lived around Tromsø where archaeological investigations have revealed a number of Viking-Age settlements.

HORIGTI or HOROTI: The Croats. Several groups of Croats were found in eastern Europe in this period. In the area between Prague and Cracow, i.e. between the Bohemians and the land of the Vistula, or of the Wislans, lived the Black Croats while the White Croats were found along the upper reaches of the river Dniester.

MÆGÞA LAND: Various interpretations have been suggested for *mægþa,* such as 'tribe' or 'magyar'. The most likely one is that it means 'of the women', and that *Mægþa land* refers to the land of Amazons. According to classical authors there was somewhere on the outskirts of the world a country populated exclusively by women; this story is found in most

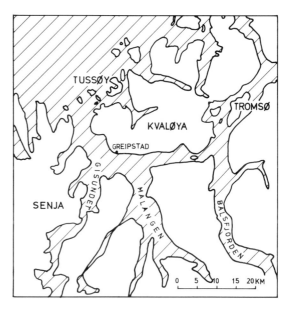

Ohthere claimed that he lived furthest to the north of all Norwegians and his home probably was in the district round the mouth of the Malang fjord. Here the northernmost evidence of agriculture and animal husbandry, dating back to about 400 AD, has been found near Greipstad on Kvaløya, and on Tussøy, twenty kilometres further to the north, a Viking-Age settlement has been excavated in recent years. The finds indicate that life here was based on fishing, hunting and animal husbandry and there was some iron production. Some imported goods have also been found which confirm the sort of contact with the outside world indicated by Ohthere's account.

descriptions of the world but the details vary considerably. A later version is found in Adam of Bremen. In the universe of the day it belongs together with the Riphaean Mountains.

MARE'S MILK: Fermented mare's milk, known as *qumys*, is an alcoholic drink of Central Asian origin. The production of it required many mares, hence its occurrence mostly among horse nomads. A detailed description of its production has been given by Guillaume de Rubruk who travelled through Central Asia 1253-55, and Adam of Bremen has heard of the drink among the Prussians (see under *Witland*): 'They eat the meat of their draught animals, and they drink their milk or blood, they are even reported to get drunk on it'.

MAROARA – MORAVIA: The Old English text says that the Moravians lived *ofer sum dæl*. This expression is ambiguous; either it could mean 'somewhat further away', 'beyond some part', or it could mean 'over a wide territory'. The interpretation of the first of these options must be that from a Saxon point of view they live beyond the Sorbs and the Bohemians. However, in the late ninth century the Greater Moravian Empire flourished, incorporating in addition to Moravia itself Bohemia and some southern Sorbian districts, Slovakia and part of Pannonia, and probably also the Wislans around the upper reaches of the Vistula. This empire was founded by Prince Rastislav (846-869) who, in order to counter Frankish influence from Bavaria and to gain Byzantine support against Louis the German (who in 862 formed an anti-Moravian alliance with Boris I of Bulgaria), called in as missionaries from Byzantium the apostles of the Slavs, Methodios and Kyrillos – the latter father of the Cyrillic alphabet. The Greater Moravian Empire reached its zenith under Rastislav's successor Svatopluk (869-894) but after his death it disintegrated under civil wars and before Magyar pressure and its last prince was killed in 906. In the last decades of the ninth century it makes good sense, therefore, to say that the Moravians 'extend over a wide territory' and the information may be perfectly up to date.

MEORE – MÖRE: A territory or province in south-east Småland. It included the southern part of the county of Kalmar and originally had its *þing* place in Dörby west of Kalmar. It was later divided into South and North Möre hundreds. The heavily wooded and trackless Småland was hardly regarded as one province in the Viking period but, as the name indicates, as a number of small territories. In addition to Möre, Värend and Finnveden may be mentioned. Blekinge, later a Danish province, and Möre, Öland and

Gotland are said to belong to the *Svear* who had their centre of gravity in Uppland while middle and western Sweden belonged to the *Götar* in Väster- and Öster-Götland. When Sweden was united into one kingdom, and whether this was due to the *Svear* or to the *Götar*, is a much-debated issue. Various overlordships no doubt existed at various times but no permanent unification was achieved until well into the eleventh century. The name *Gotland* in Wulfstan's account does not necessarily refer to the island in the Baltic. It could also refer to Östergötland to which the coast north of Möre belongs. If this is so Wulfstan is implying that shortly before 900 the *Östgötar* had been conquered by the *Svear*.

OSTI: A Wendish tribe in West Pomerania.

OSTSÆ: Seems to be not just the Baltic but to include also the Skagerrak and Kattegat. Ohthere seems to have thought of these as one sea: 'To the south of *Sciringesheal* a great sea penetrates the land; . . . This sea flows into the land for many hundred miles'.

PULGARA LAND: Bulgaria. The Protobulgarians were a Turko-Tartar people living in south Russia, along the lower reaches of the Don and on the Crimea. In the seventh century they left before the Khazars, one part going northeast and settling in the district round the lower Kama and the middle Volga, another going to the west and south where they crossed the Danube and subjugated the Slavonic population living south of its lower reaches. In the following centuries the Bulgarians were assimilated to the native Slavs and during the ninth century their empire was constantly expanding, so that under Czar Boris I (852-889) it included all of present day Romania, parts of southern Russia, Hungary as far as the river Tisza, and parts of Serbia, Macedonia and Albania. This empire frequently caused the Byzantines considerable concern.

From a Carinthian point of view Bulgaria lay beyond an uninhabited district and this was probably true in the ninth century. In 569 the Mongol Avars had conquered present day Hungary and brought the surrounding districts under their sway; they kept this until Charlemagne beat them in 796. In 883 Prince Svatopluk of Greater Moravia invaded Pannonia and annexed it to his empire, and the next year the East Frankish annals of Fulda record that the land beyond the river

Raba lay waste after this. Between the Danube and the Tisza were the Avar wilds, later known as the Hungarian *puszta;* another contemporary author speaks about the wilds of the Pannonians and the Avars. This vacuum was not filled until shortly before 900 when the Magyars invaded Europe and settled in Hungary.

RIFFEN MOUNTAINS: The Riphaean Mountains, imagined since Homer to be located north of the known parts of Europe. They were gusty and ever snowy and from them blew the North Wind. As knowledge of Europe increased these mountains were pushed further and further north and into Russia, beyond equally mysterious Scythia but they are found on maps until modern times. To Adam of Bremen they formed the northern boundary of Norway and Sweden and like his classical exempla he peoples them with terrible monsters, Cyclopes, etc. It is important to notice them in this context because they point to the sources of the information: it comes from books, not from personal experience. When these books are not telling sheer fable they may record facts applicable three or four centuries earlier but not to the ninth century.

SCRIDEFINNAS: The term normally used by Latin authors to designate the Lapps. Procopius mentions the *Skrithifinnoi* in the sixth century and they are also mentioned by Jordanes and Paulus Diaconus. Note that the term occurs in the introduction, not in Ohthere's account. There they are called *Finnas.*

SERMENDE: The Sarmatians, originally a central Asian steppe people which in the third century BC penetrated south Russia and subjugated the Scythians, another central Asian nomadic people that had conquered the region five centuries earlier. Later the name became a very imprecise designation for the population of central Russia.

SILLENDE: Over the years there has been some difference of opinion over the interpretation of this designation. Some have thought it meant Sjælland (Zealand), others that it meant the southern part of Jutland, roughly North Schleswig. On the basis of Ohthere's text Sjælland is a possible interpretation and although North Schleswig has been preferred for a long time by most, Dr Uwe Schnall has recently argued that

Sjælland should be restored to favour. Dr Schnall assumes that Viking-Age navigation followed well-determined routes and that Ohthere's account is intended as a practical description of his route for the use of others who wished to follow in his wake. Ohthere very likely was following a known route himself from *Sciringesheal* to Hedeby but his account of the journey could hardly serve anyone as a guide. As pointed out in the introduction it has been shaped and edited very much from an English point of view and with an English audience in mind, and it is so imprecise that it could hardly be of any practical value for navigation in Danish waters. It must be fairly unimportant for someone following the coast of Halland southwards to know that Jutland is on his starboard side miles out of sight. Dr Schnall pleads that it would be remarkable if Sjælland, 'that ancient centre of the Danish dynasty', should go unmentioned in an account like this but this seems to imply a revival of old notions of a powerful dynasty at Lejre, long since abandoned by most scholars. They cannot support an argument in favour of Sjælland and a linguistic analysis of the name provides no conclusive argument either.

Apart from the fact that going south *Sillende* follows Jutland, another reason for identifying it with North Schleswig is that the name occurs in the form *Sinlende* in the Frankish annals for 815 and there is no possible doubt that there South Jutland is meant. The emperor Louis the Pious was backing the aspirations of one Harald to the Danish throne and to support him the Saxon counts and their Abodrite allies crossed the river Eider, separating Holstein from Schleswig, and thereby entered the Danish province *Sinlendi*. From the Eider they could march seven days before reaching the shore of the ocean, and since Godfred's sons had escaped to an island they could do nothing about them and had to return.

Neither can it be explained away, as Dr Schnall attempts to do, that the author inserts a statement that the Angles lived in these districts before migrating to England. Our knowledge of the continental homelands of the Angles is imprecise and so was that of the author of Ohthere's account but he believed firmly that it was in Angeln because Bede says so. Therefore, when he says the Angles lived in *Sillende* before their migration he must have identified it with Schleswig. He clearly does so, too, when he first mentions *Ongle* and *Sillende* as the northwestern neighbours of the Old Saxons.

SURPE: The Sorbs, a Wendish tribe living in the district around the rivers Saale, Mulde, and the middle Elbe, between the towns Leipzig, Wittenberg, and Magdeburg, to the northeast of the *Sysyle* and the *Dalamentsan*. Their language, Lausitz Wendish, which resembles Czech closely, is still spoken in some parts of East as well as West Germany, particularly round the town of Cottbus and Bautzen in East Germany, and there is a Sorb literature.

SWÆFAS: The inhabitants of the former duchy of Swabia. The *Suebi* themselves had settled north and south of Lake Constance *c.*100 BC and in the third century AD they were joined by the *Alamanni* who amalgamated with them. Hence, Swabia was also called Alamannia, which in French became the name of all Germany. In the ninth century Swabia was part of East Frankia.

SYSYLE: The Siusli, a Wendish tribe living in the area around the river Mulde between Leipzig and Wittenberg. In the 870s they were on hostile terms with the Franks and the emperor Charles the Bald repeatedly subjugated them.

TERFINNAS: A Lappish tribe living in the Kola peninsula. Unlike the Beormas they were not farmers but hunters and fishers only.

TRUSO: A port in the Vistula delta, probably identical with later Elbing/Elblag. It is true that nothing has been excavated here that matches the remains known from other ports of that period but in the vicinity several Viking-Age finds have been made, and in the town itself a grave-field with a strong Scandinavian admixture has been excavated. Its situation at the mouth of the Vistula was very favourable for trade, this river leading deep into Eastern Europe. From its sources there is only a short distance to the Dniester by which the Black Sea and Byzantium could be reached. It was also possible via the Pripet to reach the Dnieper and Kiev, and on the upper reaches of the Vistula lay Cracow, an important trading centre from which there was a route to Prague.

ÞYRINGAS: The Thuringians, a Germanic tribe which in the sixth century formed a great realm bounded on the north by the Elbe, on the south by the Danube. This was conquered by an alliance of Franks and Saxons, the Franks taking the southern parts of it, the Saxons the northern parts. From then Thuringia formed the district between the Harz and Thüringerwald and the rivers Saale and Werra. In the ninth century Thuringia formed part of East Frankia.

WENDS: The *Wineda* or *Weonod* of the Old English text is a collective name used in German and the Scandinavian languages for a number of West Slavonic peoples.

WHALING: North Norwegian finds from the Viking period and the preceding centuries show that whales played an important role in daily life. Many different tools were made of whalebone, and although this material could have come from stranded whales there is no reason to doubt that whaling proper took place both on the open sea and in fjords and coves where the whales were driven ashore. On the Faroes the traditional hunting of pilot whales, the *Grindadrap*, still survives. If Ohthere was able with five companions to kill sixty whales in two days they must have been small whales like pilot whales whose maximum length is seven metres. Until the introduction of explosives in the late nineteenth century the capture of large whales, such as the Greenland whale, required much more time and many more men.

It is possible, though, that Ohthere is in fact claiming to have killed sixty walruses, not sixty whales, in two days. This would be quite possible. The text is ambiguous at this point, and the interrogator's understanding of this information may well have been incomplete. Ohthere is actually explaining about the walruses and their valuable teeth and strong hide, for whose sake he had travelled north, when for the sake of comparison some information about the size of whales in his homeland is inserted. It makes sense, therefore, to read the last sentence as a reference to the original subject, the walruses in the White Sea and their teeth.

WILTE: The Wilti, a Wendish tribe occupying the land south of the Abodriti between the rivers Elbe and Oder. A branch were the *Hæfeldan*, the Havolans, occupying the Havel valley. In the late tenth century they amalgamated with a number of other tribes, and this amalgamation became known as the *Lutici*.

WISLE LAND: The land of the Vistula was occupied by the Wislans who lived along the upper reaches of the Vistula with their centre at Cracow. In the middle of the tenth century they were one of a number of tribes united under the leadership of the Polonians into what became Poland but in the ninth century they were probably part of the Greater Moravian kingdom which reached its zenith under King Svatopluk (870-894), a contemporary of Alfred the Great.

WITLAND: The area between the Rivers Vistula and Memel, later known as East Prussia. The inhabitants were called *aisti* or *prusi*, Prussians – a hundred years later the Jewish merchant Ibrahim ibn Ya'qub called them *burus* – and they belonged to the Baltic ethnic group which also included Lithuanians, Latvians, Jatvingians and several minor tribes. The *Aisti* should not be confused with the Estonians living in Estonia who belong to the Finno-Ugrian ethnic group and speak a non-Indo-European language. The language of the Baltic group is Indo-European but not Slavonic.

Select Bibliography

S. B. Greenfield and F. C. Robinson, *A Bibliography of Publications on Old English Literature to the end of 1972* (Toronto, 1980).

D. Barrington, *The Anglo-Saxon Version from the Historian Orosius by Ælfred the Great. Together with an English Translation from the Anglo-Saxon* (London, 1773).

H. Sweet, *King Alfred's Orosius*, Early English Text Society, Original Series 79 (London, 1883).

J. Bosworth, *A Description of Europe and the Voyages of Ohthere and Wulfstan* . . . (London, 1885).

A. Campbell, ed. *The Tollemache Orosius (British Museum Additional MS 47967)*, Early English Manuscripts in Facsimile iii, (Copenhagen, 1953).

J. M. Bately, ed. *The Old English Orosius*, Early English Text Society, Supplementary Series 6 (Oxford, 1980).

Adam of Bremen, *Gesta Hammaburgensis Ecclesiae Pontificum* ed. W. Trillmich and R. Buchner, *Quellen des 9. und 11. Jahrhunderts zur Geschichte der hamburgischen Kirche und des Reiches* (Darmstadt, 1961).

S. Allott, ed. *Alcuin of York* . . . (York, 1974).

J. M. Bately, 'King Alfred and the Latin MSS of Orosius' History', *Classica et Mediaevalia* xxii (1961) 69-105.

J. M. Bately, 'The relationship between geographical information in the Old English Orosius and Latin texts other than Orosius', *Anglo-Saxon England* i (1972) 45-62.

J. Beckwith, *Ivory Carvings in Early Medieval England* (London, 1972).

A. L. Binns, 'Ohtheriana VI: Ohtere's Northern Voyage', *English and Germanic Studies* vii (1961) 43-52.

A. L. Binns, 'The Navigation of Viking Ships round the British Isles', *Proceedings of the Fifth Viking Congress* (Torshavn, 1968) 103-117.

A. L. Binns, 'The ships of the Vikings, were they "Viking ships"?', *Proceedings of the Eighth Viking Congress* (Odense, 1981) 287-294.

A. L. Binns, *Viking Voyagers* (London, 1980).

C. Blindheim, 'The market place in Skiringssal', *Acta Archaeologica* xxxi (1960) 83-100.

C. Blindheim, 'Kaupang in Skiringssal. A Norwegian port of trade from the Viking Age', *Vor-und Frühformen der europäischen Stadt im Mittelalter* 2, ed. H. Jankuhn, W. Schlesinger, H. Steuer, (Göttingen, 1975) 40-57.

A. W. Brøgger and H. Shetelig, *The Viking Ships* (Oslo, 1951).

A. E. Christensen, *Boats of the North*, Den Norske Samlaget, (Oslo, 1968).

O. Crumlin-Pedersen and R. Finch, *From Viking Ship to Victory* (National Maritime Museum Greenwich, 1977).

R. Derolez, 'The orientation system in the Old English Orosius', *England before the Conquest*, ed. P. Clemoes and K. Hughes, (Cambridge, 1971) 253-68.

R. Ekblom, 'Ohtere's voyage from Skiringssal to Hedeby', *Studia Neophilologica* xii (1939-40) 177-90.

R. Ekblom, 'Alfred the Great as geographer', *Studia Neophilologica* xiv (1941-2) 115-44.

R. Ekblom, 'Kıng Alfred, Ohtere and Wulfstan', *Studia Neophilologica* xxxii (1960) 3-13.

A. Ellegard, 'The Old Scandinavian system of orientation', *Studia Neophilologica* xxxii (1960) 241-248.

C. E. Fell, trans. *Egils saga* (London, 1975).

C. E. Fell, 'Unfrið: an approach to a definition', *Saga-Book of the Viking Society for Northern Research* xxi, 1-2 (1982-3) 85-100.

P. Herfert, 'Frühmittelalterliche Bootsfunde in Ralswiek, Kr. Rügen', *Ausgrabungen und Funde* xiii (1968) 211-222.

J. Herrmann, 'Ein neuer Bootsfund im Seehandelsplatz Ralswiek auf Rügen', *Ausgrabungen und Funde* xxvi, 3 (1981) 145-58.

P. Humbla and L. von Post, *Galtabäcksbåten och tidigt båtbyggeri i Norden*, Göteborgs kungl. vetenskaps-och vitterhets-samhälles handlingar, 5th series A, vi, 1 (Göteborg, 1937).

H. Jankuhn, *Haithabu. Ein Handelsplatz der Wikingerzeit* 6th ed. (Neumünster, 1976).

G. Johnston, trans. *The Saga of Gisli* (London, 1963).

S. Laing, trans. *Snorri Sturluson: Heimskringla* (rev. ed. London, 1964).

E. Liggins, 'The authorship of the Old English Orosius', *Anglia* lxxxviii (1970) 289-322.

J. Linderski, 'Alfred the Great and the tradition of ancient geography', *Speculum* xxxix (1964) 434-39.

M. Magnusson and H. Pálsson, trans. *Njál's saga* (London, 1960).

S. McGrail, 'Ships, shipwrights and seamen' in *The Viking World* by J. Graham-Campbell (London, 1980) 36-63.

L. Musset, *Les Invasions: Le second assaut contre l'Europe chrétienne (VIIe-XIe siècles)* (Paris, 1965).

O. Olsen and O. Crumlin-Pedersen *Five Viking ships from Roskilde fjord* (Roskilde, 1978).

O. Olsen and O. Crumlin-Pedersen, 'The Skuldelev Ships I' *Acta Archaeologica* xxix (Copenhagen, 1958) 161-175.

O. Olsen and O. Crumlin-Pedersen, 'The Skuldelev Ships II' *Acta Archaeologica* xxxviii (Copenhagen, 1968) 73-175.

G. Owen, 'Wynflæd's wardrobe', *Anglo-Saxon England* viii (1979) 195-222.

A. Pedersen, *Rosmarus: En beretning om hvalrossens liv og historie* (Copenhagen, 1951).

E. Roesdahl, *Viking Age Denmark* (London, 1980).

A. S. C. Ross, *The Terfinnas and Beormas of Ohthere*, 2nd ed. Viking Society for Northern Research (London, 1981).

P. H. Sawyer, *Kings and Vikings* . . . (London, 1981).

U. Schnall, 'Der Schiffahrtsweg von Skiringssal/Kaupang nach Haithabu in der fruhen Wikingerzeit', *Deutsches Schiffahrtsarchiv* iv (1981) 169-182.

Sir Frank Stenton, ed. *The Bayeux Tapestry* (London, 1957).

W. C. Stokoe, 'On Ohthere's *steorbord*', *Speculum* xxxii (1957) 299-306.

R. W. Unger, *The Ship in the Medieval Economy 600–1600* (London, 1980)

I. Whitaker, 'Ohthere's account reconsidered', *Arctic Anthropology* xviii (1981) 1-10.

I. Whitaker, 'Scridefinnas in *Widsiδ*, *Neophilologus* lxvi (1982) 602-8.

D. Whitelock, 'The Prose of Alfred's Reign', in *Continuations and Beginnings* ed. E. G. Stanley (London, 1966) 67-103.

PRINTED BY
WILLIAM SESSIONS LTD.
THE EBOR PRESS
YORK
ENGLAND